Royal Copley
(plus Royal Windsor and Spaulding)
Book I

Joe Devine
Leslie C. & Marjorie A. Wolfe

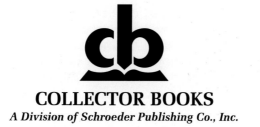

COLLECTOR BOOKS
A Division of Schroeder Publishing Co., Inc.

The current values in this book should be used only as a guide. They are not intended to set prices, which vary from one section of the country to another. Auction prices as well as dealer prices vary greatly and are affected by condition as well as demand. Neither the author nor the publisher assumes responsibility for any losses that might be incurred as a result of consulting this guide.

Please address all correspondence to:
Joseph M. Devine
1411 3rd Street
Council Bluffs, Iowa 51503-6805

Searching For A Publisher?

We are always looking for knowledgeable people considered to be experts within their fields. If you feel that there is a real need for a book on your collectible subject and have a large comprehensive collection, contact Collector Books.

Collector Books
P. O. Box 3009
Paducah, Kentucky 42002-3009

Printed in the U.S.A. by Image Graphics Inc., Paducah KY

Contents

Dedication

This book is graciously dedicated to
Marjorie A. Wolfe
In loving memory of her husband
Leslie C. Wolfe
1918 – 1987

Without their dedication and determination, the story of the Spaulding China Company would never have been told. They have earned and deserve the credit for this story.

Joseph M. Devine

Leslie C. Wolfe and Marjorie A. Wolfe, a husband and wife team, were born and reared in Illinois. For many years they studied and collected American glass and pottery. Both held graduate degrees and devoted their lives to educational and religious vocations.

For many years they were collectors of pattern glass, art glass, Greentown Glass, carnival glass, and Depression glass. Leslie was one of the early collectors of carnival glass, and became a recognized authority in the field. He was co-founder of the National Society of Carnival Glass Collectors and founder of the International Carnival Glass Association.

Both were widely known for their promotion of American glass and pottery. They were serious collectors of all the products of the Spaulding China Company of Sebring, Ohio. In addition they were collectors of Blue Ridge China, Homer Laughlin China, Abingdon Pottery, Hall China teapots, Shawnee Pottery, Red Wing Pottery, and Hull's Little Red Riding Hood.

About the Author

Joe Devine lives in Iowa. He is a retired fire captain having served over 23 years as a member of the Council Bluffs Fire Department. He is a serious collector of all Spaulding China Company products. He is an advisor to *Schroeder's Antiques Price Guide, Garage Sale and Flea Market Annual,* and is the Spaulding China Company consultant to the *Official Price Guide to Pottery and Porcelain, Eighth Edition,* by Harvey Duke.

Preface

As time goes on, the name SPAULDING will become one of the jewels in the crown of Sebring. Long a center for the production of pottery and china, Sebring, Ohio, bears a name synonymous with that of Zanesville, Roseville, and Crooksville.

The Spaulding China Company was organized in 1941 with actual production beginning in 1942. Of the many people associated with Spaulding, the name Morris Feinberg stands out. From 1941 to 1957 and during the time of liquidation, he was both the president and guiding spirit of the Spaulding operation.

Spaulding's success can be attributed to their motto, "Gift Shop Merchandise at Chain Store Prices." It was Spaulding that revolutionized the era of chain store taste for ceramics.

This book will deal mainly with Royal Copley with some emphasis on Royal Windsor and items marked Spaulding. Approximately 85% of everything made at Spaulding was Royal Copley.

Without a doubt most of the items produced at Spaulding will soon become collector items and prized by the many collectors across the country. It is the purpose and intent of this book to reveal the beauty, color, style, and design of all that belonged to Spaulding.

It is also our desire to provide a book that will be helpful for both collectors and dealers. We are taking the liberty of showing items made in as many colors as possible. This will be very helpful in ordering and buying.

A suggested value for pricing will be included for every item pictured in the book. We are disregarding prices that are not realistic. We do feel that in pricing there should be room for future growth. Please remember that pricing is only a guide and should not be considered as holy writ.

The Story of the Spaulding China Company

It seems strange that a company as outstanding as Spaulding China should remain for all practical purposes unknown and unheard of in all the material that has been written on Ohio pottery. Even the renowned author, Lois Lehner, mentions in one of her articles in the *Depression Glass Daze* that at one time she stood in the building where Royal Copley was made and didn't know it. Usually when someone attempts to write a book on a certain subject there is literature available from which to glean certain facts and information. We were forced to tell the story of Spaulding the hard way, to begin with nothing, and finally piece the story together bit by bit. It has been an interesting challenge and from this adventure we hope to reveal the glory that was Spaulding's. The story of Spaulding is unique in many ways as we shall endeavor to tell.

It all began at Sebring, Ohio, an area long noted for pottery and fine ceramic ware. Although Spaulding was born at Sebring it was, we might say, the "child" of Morris Feinberg. Without his guidance, foresight, and creative genius there would have been no Spaulding China Company. Here was a man who, singularly, would have been successful in any endeavor he might have chosen.

Contrary to dates and figures found elsewhere Spaulding did not begin operation until 1942. It was during the first six months of 1942 that production actually began. From a brief history of Sebring, Ohio, published in 1949 in connection with Sebring's 50th anniversary a few interesting facts are noted. The company began operation in a garage on East Ohio Avenue. Needing more room the plant moved temporarily to the abandoned plant of the Alliance Viterous China Company. Finally through the efforts of the Sebring businessmen they acquired the location of the old Sebring Rubber Company. The company installed the finest and most up-to-date machinery they could find at the time. They started with a straight tunnel kiln and a decorating kiln that fired at a lower temperature for decal and gold decorating. Due to increased demand and production, the straight tunnel kiln and decorating kiln were dismantled around 1947 or possibly 1948. With the installation of a large continuous circular kiln, they were able to operate 24 hours a day and in 10 hour cycles. They were in operation every day of the year except for a two week period. With the installation of the large continuous circular kiln, it was possible to fire about 1,500 dozen or 18,000 items per day. And with this kiln, only one firing was required.

Most people seem to believe that Sebring became a center for china and ceramic ware because of its clay. This was not the case. It was the

The Story of the Spaulding China Company

supply of coal and water that made Sebring the center it has been for so many years. The clay for the Spaulding China Company was shipped in from other states such as Georgia and Florida with a much needed No. 5 ball clay coming from England.

The officers of the Spaulding China Company were Morris Feinberg, president, Mount Vernon, New York; Irving Miller, vice president, Jamaica, Long Island, New York; Daniel Eisenberg, vice president and assistant secretary, Plainfield, New Jersey; and David Borowitz, secretary, Chicago, Illinois. The main office was located in the Empire State Building, New York City, New York.

The plant was operated by the following personnel: James G. Eardley, general manager; E. F. Cannell, production control; James Simpson, production; Albert Sines, maintenance supervisor; Clyde Hardy, decorating and design; Frank Weizenecker, quality control and shipping; Barbara Berry, office manager; Joan Haberland, billing; Margaret Kadisch, art and design; Carmen Lewis, design; and Dennie Welch, dipping.

Pearl Harbor and World War II meant the end of many ceramic items received from Japan and other places outside the United States. Because ceramics were not strategic to the war effort, all companies producing ceramics ware were given the signal to increase their production.

It seems that everything Spaulding did was carefully considered, planned, and worked out. The name for the company was given very special consideration. The name Spaulding rather than Spalding was selected as the name for the company. It was the u in the way the word was spelled that made the difference. The word Spaulding has an English air about it and carries with it a note of sophistication. And what about the words Royal Copley and Royal Windsor? They were carefully considered, also, and not "pulled out of the air" so to speak. For most people, the names Royal Copley and Royal Windsor suggest an association or connotation with royalty or something very fine. And the clever use of terms continue: Regal Assortment, Lennox Assortment, Carlton Assortment, Crown Assortment, Essex Assortment, and Oxford Assortment. These assortments were merely a grouping of certain birds, wall pockets, vases, and figurines into cartons of various kinds. They were sold this way and it was an efficient and convenient way of processing the orders. None of the cartons or assortments were opened. Thus, the assortment principle was a bit of merchandising that proved to be popular as well as profitable for the company.

The Spaulding operation was unique in many ways and this contributed greatly to the volume of sales and the popularity of the products. First of all, the operation was one that stressed the importance of design and quality. Spaulding soon learned that it didn't cost anymore to

The Story of the Spaulding China Company

make items of fine quality and design than it did to make junk. So their motto became "Gift Shop Merchandise at Chain Store Prices." It was their emphasis on design and quality that changed the taste of chain stores for ceramic ware. In fact we can say it was Spaulding that revolutionized the era of chain store taste for ceramics. And it wasn't long until competitors learned the lesson from Spaulding. Secondly, Spaulding maintained one of the cleanest and most immaculate plants of any around. All items were shipped in strawless and standard cartons that held up well and prevented damage and breakage. However, during the height of the war when the shortage of cartons was critical, many items were shipped in cartons from stores and places of business of various kinds. It wasn't unusual for many orders to be packed in cartons bearing the term "Kosher" on the outside. Thirdly, the plant was one of the most smoothly run in the country and won safety awards time and time again. The working relationship among the workers was one of which few companies could boast. The whole operation was without a doubt one of the finest and most efficient in the nation. Of all that we might say about personnel, the name James Eardley is one of the most significant in the history of the Spaulding operation. He stands among the giants of the company. Here was a man trusted completely by both his boss and his fellow workers. Morris Feinberg, the president, had the ability to select people of special talent to implement his desires, goals, and wishes. He had such confidence in James Eardley that Mr. Eardley was permitted to sign checks personally for over a million dollars at a time. That was a lot of money at the time! Very seldom does a man like that come along. Fourthly, Spaulding experienced no inventory difficulties and at all times knew exactly where they were. Due to strict inventory keeping, they were able to change production every two weeks. This was an innovation few companies were able to duplicate. It was all a part of the novel and efficient operation at Spaulding.

Mould making was a big operation at Spaulding. Altogether Spaulding had 50 casters (all men) and each one worked with 50 to 100 moulds depending on size and the number of cavities. Thus, there were times when as many as 4,000 moulds were in operation at one time. The mould department was kept busy not only making moulds for new items but replacing those in current production. After about 100 fillings most moulds were worn out and destroyed.

Another big department at Spaulding was the decorating department. There was a total of 35 decorators (all women) and it was from this department that the rich, blending colors were selected and applied.

Lamps were made at Spaulding. However, only lamp bases were made. Most of the lamps made at Spaulding were made early and were similar to the little bud vases and pitchers that started Spaulding on its way. Most of the lamps were made in various styles with floral decals. For the most part these lamp bases were made for only a few customers, the most important one being the Bradley Manufacturing Company of Chicago, of which David Borowitz, a stockholder in the Spaulding China Company, was president. Being sold and produced in this manner, paper labels as a rule were not applied. However, we have found a few of these same decal lamps bearing a lovely Spaulding paper label.

So many of the items marked "Royal Windsor" and "Spaulding" were made for the florist trade. The Planters of the Month or Books for Remembrance series are good examples. All items produced at the Spaulding plant were geared to demand, popularity, and the number of orders coming in. Royal Windsor for the most part was made later and represented only modest production. Copley was so popular and such a big item it tended to overshadow everything else that was made.

Although the quality of Royal Windsor and items marked "Spaulding" were not superior to Royal Copley, the items commanded a higher price because they were handled by department stores.

How easy the story of Spaulding China Company would have been had all items been stamped or marked with raised letters. Fortunately many items were marked, but so many left the plant with only a sticker or paper label. And over the years the labels were removed or washed off. How thankful we are that so many Copley items, Royal Windsor, and Spaulding items bear their original labels. We are conscious of the fact we are working in virgin territory and it just may be we have failed to include some items that should have been included and included some items that should not have been included. We are hoping the book will become so popular that within a matter of time we can update everything and resolve any mistakes we have made.

We are relying upon all the evidence we have gained here and there. Familiarity and study is of great help in identification and comments from collectors of long standing have been invaluable.

Without a doubt every item produced at the Spaulding plant was given a paper label. However, there is a lot of confusion concerning the paper labels. It is interesting to note that some Royal Copley items can be found with a Spaulding label and some Royal Windsor items can be found with a Royal Copley label. For the most part we have been able to identify an item by characteristics other than that of a label. With so many items being produced it is easy to see how paper labels might have ended up on the wrong item. Really, it doesn't make any difference as it all came from the same plant. However, for the most part, the right sticker did get "stuck" to the right item. Again, we want to stress the fact

The Story of the Spaulding China Company

that it was Royal Copley that was sold almost exclusively to the chain stores. Good merchandising has many fine points and there are reasons why many things are done. A name can make a lot of difference in sales. It certainly did at Spaulding. If the real truth were known it just may be that certain items sold better if a certain label were applied. The authors have taken a lot of liberty here but after all it is conceivable that the idea of "giving them what they want" is nothing more than good business.

The company prospered, growing in volume to become at its peak the second largest artware pottery in the United States.

With the end of World War II the tastes and attitudes of people began to change. About a year before the factory closed, the company, in order to meet competition and changing demands, began to produce items combined or associated with wire goods. This was the "thing" at that time.

It was during this time that most companies began to experience labor difficulties of various kinds and Spaulding was no exception. During this time of change and adjustment there was, everywhere, a deterioration of morals in business. Many stores began to cancel orders without any intention of fulfilling their part of the contract. In fact many businesses abused their supplier.

Without a doubt it was severe competition from the Japanese that hastened the decision to cease operation at Spaulding, for the Japanese were flooding the market with decorative pottery at very competitive prices. And to make it worse, wage rates in Sebring were the highest in the pottery industry in the United States.

With the approach of the sixties it was obvious the nation had entered an age and time in which the good, old established ways of doing business were gone. Morris Feinberg was a man who loved business and work; but when it reached the point of interfering with his peace of mind, he considered it time to get out of the rat race. Therefore, in 1957 he retired, but before doing so honored the orders and contracts of customers by turning them over to a near-by company, China Craft, to fill. For a period of almost two years such orders and contracts were filled. It was a rather natural kind of business arrangement as Mr. R. H. Brown, the president of China Craft, was formerly with Spaulding. Mr. R. H. Brown was not the first to leave Spaulidng to form his own company.

George Stanford, a former manager at Spaulding, left Spaulding and formed the Stanford Pottery Company. It was Stanford that made the lovely Corn pattern that is becoming popular among collectors.

Before we close the story of Spaulding, we would like to add that Irving Miller deserves a special place in the history of the Spaulding China Company. He was an early partner of Morris Feinberg. In those early

The Story of the Spaulding China Company

days while Morris was making frequent trips between New York and Sebring, it was Irving Miller who headed up the sales. Irving Miller, vice president, not only headed up sales but approved many of the items that were to go into production. He was, in our estimation, another giant in the story of Spaulding.

Spaulding was first sold to a Mr. Shiffman who was in the plumbing business. He made primarily small sinks for mobile homes but the operation was not successful. His problem was solved through the help and guidance of Morris Feinberg. There was no foreclosure but through a financial arrangement Mr. Shiffman was relieved of his obligation.

Vacant for a few years, the plant was sold in 1964 to Mr. Eugene T. Meskill, president of Holiday Designs, Inc. They made primarily canisters, cookie jars, teapots, and accessory items.

In May of 1982 the plant was sold once more to Mr. Richard C. Durstein of Pittsburgh, Pennsylvania. Mr. Meskill remained with the company for an indefinite period of time. Thus, the story of this special plant ends here. But the glory of Spaulding will ever speak to us.

11

A Broad View of Royal Copley

Royal Copley — America's latest collectible! Already, before anything has been written on the subject, the supply is rapidly disappearing from flea markets, garage sales, and those stores handling the later collectibles.

Copley entered the scene as a collectible for several reasons:

a. Its rich, blending colors and quality of design quickly caught the eye of collectors.

b. It provided a new outlet for collectors who had reached the limit with many other collectibles.

c. Prices for the most part are modest and within the reach of everyone.

d. Copley can be found with ease, although many pieces remain to be recognized.

e. Most Royal Copley items, by virtue of their style and character, have a strong personal appeal. So many of the items are associated with beautiful flowers, colorful birds, and those animals that appeal to our human emotions.

Copley was bound to catch on as some of the designers were the best in the business. They gave common production ware a sophistication afforded many of our finer wares. However, it must be pointed out that Royal Copley, although very colorful and beautifully designed, lacks the ceramic quality and individual treatment afforded the truly fine pieces. This ware was mass produced for a ready market with little or no personal treatment. Although air brushed almost exclusively, the overall results were unusually lovely and appealing.

What a pity no records were kept of the various items produced. And Spaulding had no morgue where examples of the various items produced were kept and stored. No one ever dreamed the bulk of the production lines of the Spaulding China Company would, within a matter of a few years, become prized collector items. Had it not been for the merchandising genius of Morris Feinberg, the name Royal Copley would be primarily a term unknown to anyone. Copley had an appeal that reached out and touched.

So much variety exists in Royal Copley that a collector can select any area he or she desires. There are figurines of all kinds, planters of all descriptions, vases of every design, wall planters of unbelievable quantity, and various combinations of planters and pockets made either to hang on the wall or rest on a table.

Collectors will find many colors from which to choose and some items may be found in as many as four, five, or more colors. There seems to be no limit on the number of items that are showing up. Some were made for only a short time and some were produced in very large quantities. The items produced for only a short time are the premium items of today. The practice of producing many items in pairs (male and female) did much to enhance their popularity. And many items were made to be used either as figurines or planters. As a rule, figurines and vases are prized more than planters. However, Copley seems to be an exception in this respect. The bulk of the planters are so beautifully designed they give the appearance of being figurines or artful objects. It is hard to find planters, wall pockets, and vases in good condition if they have been exposed to wet soil and stagnant water for long periods of time.

Copley's vast selection of birds did more than anything else in bringing the Royal Copley name to the average household. The popularity of Copley really began with the vast selection of birds, although a small series of decal bud vases and pitchers was the first to find favor with the general public.

Copley is subject to crazing with some items crazing more than others. Extremes in temperature, stagnant water, wet soil, and prolonged use of water over a period of time leads to more drastic crazing and spider-webbing. Many lovely items have been ruined through negligent use. Items heavily crazed and stained may be cleared up somewhat by bleaching.

As we mentioned a bit earlier the first items produced by the Spaulding China Company were a series of small pitchers and bud vases with decals of pink and blue flowers on a cream background. These items were stamped "Royal Copley" in gold letters on the bottom. However, some of these very same items can be found with a Spaulding stamp with gold lettering. However, it is safe to say that 95% of the early decal items were stamped "Royal Copley" and all with a gold stamp.

Royal Copley, the pride of Spaulding, was produced during the entire time the company was in operation and even during the time of liquidation. Although the Spaulding China Company produced three distinct lines: Royal Copley, Royal Windsor, and Spaulding, it was Royal Copley that constituted about 85% of the entire production.

Royal Copley was sold almost exclusively to the chain stores such as Woolworths, Kresges, Grants, and Murphys. Woolworth was Spaulding's biggest customer for Royal Copley.

Items marked "Royal Windsor" and "Spaulding" were primarily made for jobbers, department stores, and gift shops.

For many the term "air brushing" is not understood. It was the way in which the many colors and combinations of colors were applied to the clay figures. Instead of applying the color with a brush in the traditional

A Broad View of Royal Copley

way, the decorators used little spray guns about the size of a pen or pencil with a little container to hold the paint. Each little spray gun was attached to an air supply which enabled the decorator to control the flow of paint through little adjustable nozzles on the end of each gun. Several ladies were assigned to a table with each one performing a specific task in the total operation. Some "dotted" the eyes, some tinted the faces, and others used stencils or masks in creating the desired portions of color here and there. It was a shared operation with each person becoming very adept in her work. As we mentioned elsewhere the decorating department used only women with a certain number being assigned to each table. It was the responsibility of the person in charge of this department to produce a model for each to follow. Just think what 35 women were able to accomplish!

Spaulding produced more birds than any other single item. The bird business mushroomed as we can imagine. Mr. Feinberg estimated that as many as 500 dozen birds (6,000 birds) were made each day. He also estimated that 150,000 dozen (1,800,000 birds) were made each year. Try to imagine the number of birds produced during the entire time of Spaulding!

Without a doubt the company made more money on birds than any other single item. They sold as reasonably as 25 cents at the chain stores with the larger birds bringing more money. The birds selling for 25 cents retail were purchased wholesale at $1.80 per dozen ($.15 each).

Copley's biggest sellers were the following: birds, piggie banks, roosters, the large ducks, and the Oriental Boy and Girl wall pockets. The Oriental Boy and Girl wall pockets were marketed for three or four years when there was a "craze" for Chinese motifs in decorating.

Although Copley was designed specifically for the chain stores, there were times during the war in which some Copley items (particularly the birds) were sold to gift stores and department stores.

How to Identify Royal Copley and Distinguish It from Other Wares

What a challenge identification has become with so many of the products of the Spaulding China Company! Although we are attempting to present the full story of all those items made at Spaulding, our main concern is Royal Copley. Although Spaulding made more than Copley we can safely say that Spaulding was 85% Royal Copley.

What a simple task this book would have been had all items been marked in some way! Fortunately, a lot of Royal Copley was marked either with a gold or green stamp or the name "Royal Copley" spelled out in raised letters. Although paper labels were attached to every item leaving the factory, few have remained for purposes of identification. All in all, there are more unmarked than marked pieces of Royal Copley. However, through study, familiarity, and comparison the following guide lines have become helpful clues in the process of identification.

1. Most Royal Copley is characterized by brilliant color combinations and sparkling designs.
2. If the item appears to be cheap and gaudy one can be reasonably sure it is not Royal Copley.
3. All color and decoration is under the glaze.
4. Never is Royal Copley more than two mold.
5. If an item for its size, is thin and very light in weight, it is most likely an import or the product of some other company.
6. If a bird is heavy, glazed inside and out, and only of one color it is not a genuine piece of Royal Copley.
7. Most of the birds, with the exception of the ducks and chickens, seem to be associated, in some way, with a tree stump, limb, or knot hole.
8. Most Royal Copley is characterized by detail and novelty of design. We are using the word "most" because a lot of Copley, although pretty, is rather common. There are some very lovely floral patterns, but most of them lack botanical exactness. Therefore, we are forced to use the word "stylized" to prevent any error in identification. The real style, beauty, and detail of Royal Copley can be seen in the many human and animal faces that are found on figurines, planters, and wall pockets. Here, the designers of Royal Copley seemed to out-do themselves. The faces seem to have a personality all of their own and, in addition, they tend to bring out certain realistic human emotions.
9. Although not a hard and fast rule, the presence of parallel runners or ridges on the bottom of many of the items is one of the very im-

portant clues in identifying Royal Copley. There are exceptions, but for the most part the presence of ridges strongly suggest that the item is Copley. Great care has to be exercised because similar ridges can be found on many of the Shawnee and Hull items. However, the tendency toward ridges is not wide spread in these lines.

10. As a basic rule the Copley birds do not have totally and specifically painted-on toes or totally and specifically painted-on beaks. The beaks, if tinted, are mainly tinted on the upper portion with no specific application of color other than the general blending of body color. We must point out that a few Copley birds appear to have received some bit of hand decorating or brushing at the factory. This is the exception. If a bird has been "touched" at the factory, it is merely that of providing a few brush marks here and there. Please notice it is the non-Copley bird that has specifically and totally painted-on toes and beaks. Most Copley birds are consistently air brushed with no personal treatment or touch of any kind other than that provided by the one who sat at the decorating table.

11. Most Royal Copley items have glazed bottoms because the ridges or runners on the bottom of the items allowed them to go through the kiln firing without getting wiped off. The glaze on the ridges was wiped off as soon as an item was taken out of the glaze tub. The ridges or runners also provided strength for the item. However, many Copley items have unglazed bottoms such as the small banks, the full bodied birds, figurines, and the full bodied ducks and chickens. We realize birds are animals, too, but we are doing this for ease of understanding. If a Copley item has an unglazed bottom, it is usually hollow all the way through or has a hole or holes in the center of the base. We have found only one unglazed item that rests flat on the table without any hole or holes in the center of the base.

Labels

Royal Copley Items

Row 1: (a) 3½" x 7" Floral Arrangement Planter. Green stamp on bottom. $10.00 – 12.00.

(b) 2½" x 6¼" Sectioned Planter. Signed with raised letters on the bottom. Made in several sizes and color combinations. Identified as No. 35 on one of the company brochures. $8.00 – 10.00.

(c) and (d) 3½" Little Ribbed Planters. The only difference is color. Signed with raised letters on the bottom. $8.00 – 10.00 each.

Row 2: (a) 7" Decal Vase. Identified as No. 45 on one of the company's color charts. Paper label only. Sometimes this vase is highlighted in blue as well as a deep rose. This is the only Copley item we have that has a perfectly flat unglazed bottom without any hole in the base. $12.00 – 15.00.

(b) 6¼" Pink Beauty Vase. Gold stamp on bottom. Outlined in gold. This is the same vase as shown elsewhere but with a decal of flowers on a cream background. One of the early items. $12.00 – 14.00.

(c) 6¼" Floral Handle Vase. Gold stamp on bottom. Outlined in gold. More easily found. This is the same vase as shown elsewhere but with a floral decal on a cream background. One of the early items. $12.00 – 14.00.

Row 3: (a) and (b) 3¼" x 6" Coach Planters. Green stamp on bottom. Item (a) is a kind of beige whereas item (b) is a kind of teal. It can also be found in a deep rose or plum. $18.00 – 20.00 each.

(c) 3" Big Blossom Planter. Green stamp on bottom. It is most often found in this color. When found with a green background and yellow blossom, it is often called Daffodil by collectors. When used with the green Daffodil pitcher it gives the impression of being a part of a set. $10.00 – 12.00.

Royal Copley Items

Row 1: (a) 7" Ivy Footed Vase. Paper label only. Dark green leaves on ivory background. $10.00 – 12.00.
(b) 8" Ivy Footed Vase. Paper label only. $12.00 – 14.00.
(c) 4" Ivy Footed Planter. Paper label only. $8.00 – 10.00.

Row 2: (a) 6¼" Ivy Pillow Footed Vase. Paper label only. Pillow vases are more popular and in greater demand. $16.00 – 18.00.
(b) 4" x 7" Ivy Window Box Planter. Paper label only. $12.00 – 14.00.
(c) 6¼" Ivy Pillow Footed Vase (gold outlined). Paper label only. The gold outlined items are truly lovely and in greater demand. $26.00 – 28.00.

Row 3: (a) Handled Leaf Creamer. Green stamp on base. Made in several colors. It seems strange that a creamer and sugar were made in Royal Copley when no dinnerware was made. Height of 3". $20.00 – 24.00.
(b) and (c) 8" Daffodil Pitchers. Green stamp on bottom. The only difference between the pitchers is that of color. If there are other colors we haven't seen them. Very popular and in great demand. $55.00 – 60.00 each.
(d) Handled Leaf Sugar. Green stamp on base. Like the matching creamer in (a) it was made in several colors. $20.00 – 24.00.

Royal Copley Items

Row 1: (a), (b), and (c) 8" Floral Beauty Pitchers. Green stamp or raised letters on the bottom. Item (b) seems to be the favorite among collectors. $45.00 – 50.00 each; cobalt $60.00 – 65.00.

Row 2: (a), (b), and (c) 7" Carol's Corsage Vases. Green stamp on bottom. Listed as No. 55 on one of the color charts of the company. This item is named in honor of Carol Phillips of Marshfield, Wisconsin. $18.00 – 20.00 each.

Row 3: (a) and (b) 8" Pome Fruit Pitchers. Green stamp on the bottom. Blue $50.00 – 55.00; tan $45.00 – 50.00.
    (c) 8" Floral Elegance Vase. A collector of Copley soon realizes that beauty and design are more important than botanical exactness. This vase can be found in other colors but the cobalt seems to be the favorite among collectors. Cobalt $28.00 – 32.00.

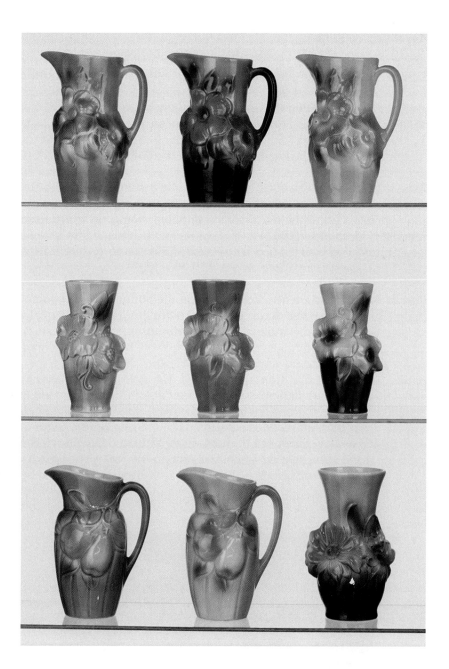

Royal Copley Items

Row 1: (a) 6¼" Two-Handled Decal Vase. Gold stamp on the bottom. $10.00 – 14.00.

(b) 6" Decal Pitcher. Gold stamp on the bottom. $12.00 – 14.00.

(c) 6¼" Decal Pitcher. Gold stamp on the bottom. $12.00 – 16.00.

(d) 6" Decal Pitcher. Gold stamp on the bottom. $12.00 – 16.00.

Row 2: (a) 6¼" Two-Handled Decal Vase. Gold stamp on the bottom. $10.00 – 14.00.

(b) 8" Two-Handled Decal Vase. Gold stamp on the bottom. $16.00 – 20.00.

(c) 6¼" Two-Handled Decal Vase. Gold stamp on the bottom. Handles are more ornate. $10.00 – 14.00.

Row 3: (a) 6" Decal Pitcher. Gold stamp on the bottom. A little harder to find with this decal. $12.00 – 16.00.

(b) 4⅛" Stub Handle Vase. Gold stamp on the bottom. It is a vase although it has the appearance of being a spoon holder or a sugar bowl without a lid. $12.00 – 15.00.

(c) and (d) 8¼" Cornucopia Vases. The gold outline makes this pair more desirable. Item (c) has "Royal Copley" in raised letters on the bottom whereas item (d) has "Spaulding China" in gold letters on the bottom. The marking on the bottom is the only difference in these vases. Finding different marks on the same item is not unusual among the many items made at Spaulding. $25.00 – 30.00 each.

Royal Copley Items

Row 1: (a), (b), (c), and (d) 5" Warblers. Green stamp or raised letters on the bottom. Identified as No. 15/2 on one of the color charts of the company. Designed for use as a bud vase. $18.00 – 20.00 each.

Row 2: (a), (b), (c), and (d) 6¼" Woodpeckers. Signed with green stamp or raised letters on the bottom. Designed for use as a planter. Wide variation in color. Item (d) is turned to show the lovely floral design on the stamp. $20.00 – 25.00 each.

Row 3: (a), (b), (c), and (d) 6¼" Tanagers. Green stamp or raised letters on the bottom of this planter. Notice the lovely color variations. Named in honor of Dr. Richard W. Pippen of Western Michigan University. $20.00 – 25.00 each.

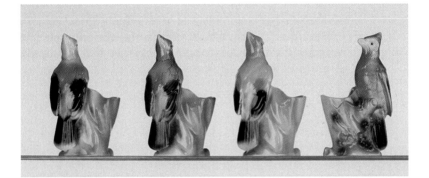

Royal Copley Items

Row 1: (a), (b), and (c) 7¼" Cockatoos. Paper label only. Full bodied. Sought after by collectors. Notice the conspicuous erectile crest. Named in honor of Dr. Lawrence B. Hunt, ornithologist, Eastern Illinois University at Charleston, Illinois. (a) and (c) $30.00 – 35.00 each; (b) $35.00 – 40.00.

Row 2: (a), (b), and (c) 8" Parrots. Note the variation in color. Item (a) is mainly yellow; item (b) is predominantly blue; and item (c) is mainly lime green. Paper label only. Full bodied. Prized by collectors. Easier to find than the cockatoos in Row 1. Named in honor of Mrs. Chris Morrow of Villa Grove, Illinois. (a) and (c) $35.00 – 40.00 each; (b) $40.00 – 45.00.

Row 3: (a) and (b) Cockatoos that we are naming Big Cockatoos. Height of 8¼". Item (a) has a body that is mainly dark green in color whereas item (b) has a body color that is primarily pink or deep rose. Raised letters on the bottom. Full bodied. Named in honor of Dr. Iain Paul of Illinois. $40.00 – 45.00 each.

Royal Copley Items

Row 1: (a), (b), (c), and (d) 6½" Thrushes. Full bodied. Paper label only. We must remember that the Copley birds were not designed for overall accuracy. It appears from time to time, according to our neighbor, Dr. George Godfrey, assoc. prof. scientist at the Illinois Natural History Survey that the artist or designer was endeavoring to capture the overall appearance or Gestalt of certain groups of birds. Therefore the figurines have resemblances of particular orders or families but do not depict actual species. Variation in color. $20.00 – 24.00 each.

Row 2: (a), (b), (c), (d), and (e) 6½" Larks. Full bodied. Paper label only. Great variation in color. Identified as No. 21 on one of the color charts. $20.00 – 24.00 each.

Row 3: (a), (b), (c), (d), and (e) 6¼" Wrens. Paper label only. Notice the wide variation in color. The wrens add a lot of color to any bird collection. $20.00 – 24.00 each.

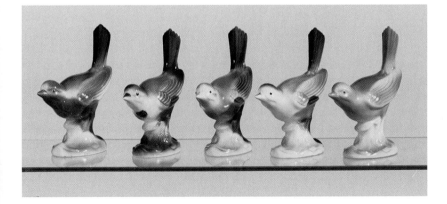

31

Royal Copley Items

Row 1: (a), (b), and (c) 7" Swallow with Extended Wings. Full bodied. Paper label only. Identified as No. 35 in the Regal Assortment of Copley birds. Rare. Shown in the three color variations in which they were made. $80.00 – 90.00 each.

Row 2: (a), (b), (c), and (d) 8" Swallows. Full bodied. Paper label only. Great variation in color. Notice that some face to the left and others face to the right. $25.00 – 30.00 each.

Row 3: (a), (b), (c), and (d) 8" color variations of the Titmouse. Notice that item (b) has been given some fancy treatment and it is all under the glaze. We are finding the same bit of decorating on other birds although it was not normally done. Full bodied. Paper label only. Named in honor of Sharon and Bob Huxford, renowned pottery authors, of Covington, Indiana. $25.00 – 35.00 each.

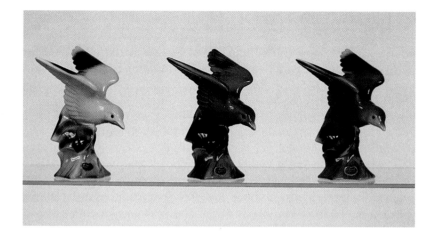

Royal Copley Items

Row 1: (a), (b), and (c) 5" Kingfishers. Shown in the three color variations in which they were made. Very colorful and hard to
find. $45.00 – 50.00 each.

Row 2: (a), (b), and (c) 5" Kingfishers. These are the mates to the birds
shown above in Row 1. $45.00 – 50.00 each.

Row 3: (a), (b), and (c) Variations in color of what we must refer to as
wren-like birds. For the sake of reference we are calling these
lovely items Double Birds on Tree Stump. Paper label only.
Full bodied. Prized highly. This bird was identified as No. 17
in the Regal Assortment. $40.00 – 45.00 each.

Royal Copley Items

Row 1: (a), (b), and (c) 8" Gulls. Items (b) and (c) have wings that are molded to the base. Item (a) is referred to as an Applied Wing Gull. Paper label only. Harder to find, especially item (a) $70.00 – 75.00; (b) and (c) $40.00 – 45.00 each.

Row 2: (a) and (c) from Row 1 above are turned to show the difference in how these birds were made.

Row 3: (a), (b), (c), and (d) 8" Flycatchers. Paper label only. Notice the added hand painting of the toes and back of neck on item (c). A favorite among collectors. $40.00 – 45.00 each.

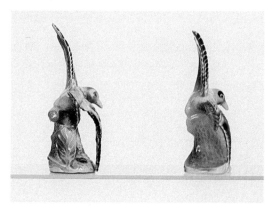

Royal Copley Items

Row 1: (a), (b), (c), (d), and (e) 4½" Vireos. Paper label only. Notice the wide variation in color. Please remember that accuracy of color wasn't given much consideration. They were designed to be colorful and to sell well. $12.00 – 16.00 each.

Row 2: (a), (b), (c), (d), and (e) 5" Larks. Paper label only. The bird rests on a very fancy stump. Full bodied. $12.00 – 16.00 each.

Row 3: (a), (b), (c), (d), and (e) 5" Sparrows. Paper label only. Wide variation in color which adds to the beauty of a Copley bird collection. $12.00 – 16.00 each.

Royal Copley Items

The Copley birds, beautiful and lovely as they are, lack exactness as far as color, size, and distinguishing characteristics are concerned. Many were copied from European birds which differ greatly from the American species. Only with the help of an outstanding ornithologist were we able to give these lovely creatures a suitable name.

Row 1: (a) and (c) 5½" Nuthatch Vase or Planter. Paper label only. Three runners. The design of the stump helps to identify this item. $30.00 – 35.00 each.

(b) 6½" Goldfinch on Stump Planter. Paper label only. Three runners. Not too difficult to find. $30.00 – 35.00.

Row 2: (a) and (c) 5¼" Hummingbird on Flower Planters. Paper label only. The blue bird is harder to find. (a) $55.00 – 60.00; (c) $70.00 – 75.00 each.

(b) 8" Birdhouse with Bird Planter. One of the premium items and a favorite with collectors. Paper label only. $100.00 – 110.00.

Row 3: (a) 6½" Big Apple and Finch Planter. Paper label only. $30.00 – 35.00.

(b) 7½" Fancy Finch or Finch-like Bird on Tree Stump Planter. Paper label only. Another one of Copley's top of the line items. $65.00 – 70.00.

(c) 6¼" Wren on Tree Stump Planter. Paper label only. $30.00 – 35.00.

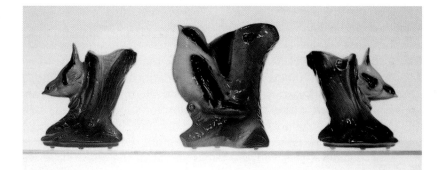

Royal Copley Items

Row 1: (a), (b), and (c) 8" Rooster Banks. As you can see, items (a) and (b) were made in two color variations. Item (b), with the brown breast, is very hard to find. Item (c), with the cobalt tail, was made only in this color combination. These banks may be found marked on the bottom: "Chicken Feed, Reg. U. S. Pat. Office, Vic Moran, Bradford, PA." Of all of the collectors that have these banks and all of the ones I have seen, none has ever been found with a Royal Copley label which leads me to believe, and this opinion is shared by many longtime collectors, that these items may have been produced on a contract basis. $65.00 – 75.00 each.

Row 2: (a), (b), and (c) 8" Rooster Banks. The coin slot is at the top of the tail. At the base on the front are the words, "Chicken Feed." These three solid-colored banks with gold trim were more than likely produced by the Stanford Pottery Company also of Sebring, Ohio, as these are standard colors they used on figurines, etc. As a matter of fact, the only labels that have been found on these banks, either solid color or the colors in Row 1, have been Stanford labels. No price available.

Row 3: (a) and (b) 8" Rooster and Wheelbarrow Planters. Notice that the handles of the wheelbarrow on item (a) rest on a bench while the handles of item (b) rest on a barrel. Item (a) is a rare item in itself, but item (b) is, so far, the only one that has been reported. Found with a paper label only. A very popular item. (a) $135.00 – 150.00; (b) Too rare to price. Item (b) shown in honor of the late Roy Wooldridge.

Royal Copley Items

Row 1: (a) 6½" Royal Copley "Banty" Rooster Figurine. Not many of these roosters have surfaced to date and no matching hen has been found. Paper label only. $50.00 – 60.00.

(b) 7" Royal Copley Rooster Figurine. With the exception of the tail feathers, this rooster resembles the Rooster on the Wheelbarrow shown on the previous page. This is the only example found to date. Too rare to price.

Row 2: (a) Small Copley 5½" Hen No. 1. Paper label only. The small chickens are harder to find. $30.00 – 35.00.

(b) Small Copley 6" Rooster No. 1. Paper label only. This rooster and its mate above appear to be standing in straw. This is the clue in matching this pair. $30.00 – 35.00.

(c) Small Royal Copley 6" Hen No. 2. Paper label only. $35.00 – 40.00.

(d) Small Copley Rooster 6¼" No. 2. Paper label only. This rooster, like its mate, has a base similar to that of the large Copley rooster and hen. $35.00 – 40.00.

Row 3: (a) 7" Large Royal Copley Hen. Paper label only. Notice that the feet do not show in the large chickens. Color will vary with the tops of tail feathers, either solid black or black and green. $40.00 – 45.00.

(b) 8" Large Copley Rooster. Paper label only. The feet do not show. Color will vary with some of the tail feathers showing either more green or more brown. Rooster is easier to find than the hen. $40.00 – 45.00.

(c) 8" Large Royal Copley Rooster. The only difference is that of color. $40.00 – 45.00.

Royal Copley Items

Row 1: (a) 6½" Royal Copley Fighting Cock Planter. Paper label only. Two runners. $45.00 – 50.00.
(b) and (c) 5½" Walking Rooster Planter/Wall Pockets. Signed with raised letters on the back. The white one is harder to find. (b) $45.00 – 50.00; (c) $40.00 – 45.00.

Row 2: (a) 7⅛" Royal Copley Low Tail Common Rooster Planter. Paper label only. Two runners. $30.00 – 35.00.
(b) and (c) 7¾" High Tail Common Rooster Planters. Signed on the bottom with raised letters. Only difference is color variation. $30.00 – 35.00 each.

Row 3: (a) 8½" Rooster Planter. Paper label only. Two runners. $40.00 – 45.00.
(b) 8" Hen Planter. Paper label only. Two runners. $40.00 – 45.00.
(c) 7⅛" Rooster Vase. Paper label only. Two runners. The high flowing tail adds to the beauty of this vase. $40.00 – 45.00.

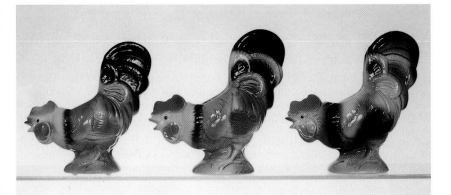

Royal Copley Items

Row 1: (a) 3¾" Duck and Wheelbarrow Planter. Paper label only. This item, like all the action items, is very popular. $18.00 – 20.00.

(b) 6¾" Duck and Mail Box Planter. Paper label only. U.S. Mail appears on the mail box. A rare item. $75.00 – 85.00.

Row 2: (a) 7¼" Mature Wood Duck. Paper label only. Rather hard to find. Designed as a planter. $35.00 – 40.00.

(b) 5½" Wood Duck. Paper label only. Rather hard to find. Designed as a planter. $20.00 – 25.00.

(c) 5" Duck Eating Grass. Paper label only. Easy to find. $18.00 – 20.00.

Row 3: (a) 5" Kinglet. Paper label only. Easy to find. Aren't the Copley birds lovely? However, identification is extremely difficult as they were not designed to be exact in every way. And we must ignore color a great deal of the time. $18.00 – 20.00.

(b) and (c) 5" Bunting Planters. Signed with raised letters on the back. Easy to find. This planter was listed as No. 69 in the Lenox Assortment. We are listing this item in honor of Ed Lohr of Villa Grove, Illinois. $30.00 – 35.00 each.

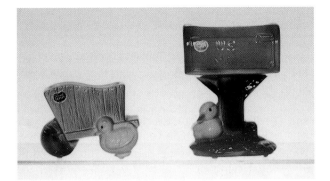

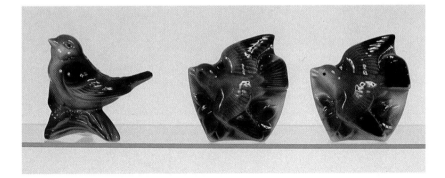

Royal Windsor Items

Row 1: (a) and (b) Royal Windsor Chickens. Rooster is 7" and the hen 6½". This pair with their stucco glazing may or may not have been made by China Craft. $50.00 – 60.00 pair.

Row 2: (a) and (b) Royal Windsor Chickens. Rooster is 7" and the hen 6½". The rooster is similar in design to the Royal Copley "Banty" Rooster shown on page 44. $60.00 – 70.00 pair.
(c) 6⅝" Royal Windsor Rooster. A smaller version of item (b). $30.00 – 35.00.

Row 3: (a) and (b) Royal Windsor Chickens. Rooster is 7⅛" and the hen is 6¼". Both have "U.S.A." impressed on the rim of the base. $80.00 – 90.00 pair.
(c) and (d) Small Royal Windsor Mallards. The Drake is 5¾" and the hen is 4⅛". Both have "U.S.A." impressed on the rim of the base. $150.00 – 175.00 pair.

Royal Copley Items

Row 1: (a) 8" Mallard Duck on Copley Stump. This item can be used either as a vase or planter. Paper label only. $40.00 – 45.00.
(b) 8" Mallard Duck Planter. Paper label only. $15.00 – 20.00.
(c) 7" Mallard Duck Figurine. Paper label only. The figurine is harder to find than the planter. $20.00 – 25.00.

Row 2: (a) 5¼" Sitting Mallard Hen Planter. Found with a Royal Windsor label. Watch out for copies of this one. When you see the real one with its beautiful color combination and quality, you will have no trouble spotting the fake. $45.00 – 50.00.
(b), (c), and (d) Three ducks that make up the smoking set. The larger one (3") serves as a cigarette holder and the two smaller ones (2") as ashtrays. Paper label only. $50.00 – 60.00 set.

Row 3: (a) 5" Sitting Mallard Drake Planter. Paper label only. Three runners. Mate to item (a) above in Row 2. $30.00 – 35.00.
(b) 8" Split Neck Mallard Duck Planter. Harder to find. Three runners. $20.00 – 25.00.
(c) 8" Mallard Duck Planter. Paper label only. Only difference between these two mallards and those above in Row 1 is that of the breast color and, like item (c) above, it may be found in a figurine. $20.00 – 25.00.

Royal Copley Items

Row 1: (a) 8" "Mill" Plaque Planter. One of the surprises in Copley! It is signed in script in lower left corner. "The Mill," Amsterdam, Holland, by Jacob van Ruysdael. Made to hang or rest on a table. "Royal Copley" in raised letters on the back. Designed by Anthony Priolo. $60.00 – 70.00.

(b) A similar item without any decal. It is most likely a blank. $40.00 – 50.00.

(c) 8" Plaque Planter. This one reads "Turner Crossing the Brook" Amsterdam, Holland. Same characteristics as items (a) and (b). $60.00 – 70.00.

Row 2: (a) 7½" Deer Open Vase-Planter. One of the five items in the Essex Assortment. Paper label only. $20.00 – 25.00.

(b) 7¼" Bird in Flight Open Vase-Planter. Paper label only. $25.00 – 30.00.

(c) 5¾" Open Fish Vase-Planter. Paper label only. Wide variation in color with other colors shown elsewhere. This item is highlighted in gold which makes it special. $25.00 – 30.00.

Row 3: (a) 6¾" Fruit Plate Plaque Planter. Signed with raised letters and made either to hang or rest on a table. Included in the Oxford Assortment. $30.00 – 35.00.

(b) 6¾" Copley Hen Plaque Planter. Signed with raised letters and made to hang or rest on a table. $40.00 – 45.00.

(c) 6¾" Copley Rooster Plaque Planter. Same description holds as the hen planter above. $40.00 – 45.00.

Royal Copley Items

Row 1: (a) 5½" Oriental Style Footed Fish Vase or Planter. The two fish appear only on the front side and are mainly blue and pink in color. Paper label only. $12.00 – 15.00.

(b) 8" Cylindrical Fish Vase. The two fish appear only on the front. Vase is signed with raised letters on the bottom. This vase is beautifully outlined in gold. The fish are green and light brown in color. It was one of the five items in the Essex Assortment. $20.00 – 24.00.

(c) 5" Half-circle Fish Vase or Planter. Paper label only. Fish are pink and blue. $25.00 – 30.00.

Row 2: (a) and (b) 5¼" Open Fish Vase-Planters. Paper label only. The only difference is color. This vase was listed as No. 660 in the Essex Assortment. $20.00 – 24.00 each.

Row 3: (a) and (c) 5½" Oriental Style Footed Dragon Vases. Paper label only. The only difference is that of color. $12.00 – 15.00 each.

(b) 7" Cylindrical Fish Vase. Color and design are very similar to item (c) in Row 1. This same pattern can be found on a 3¾" oval planter. $20.00 – 25.00.

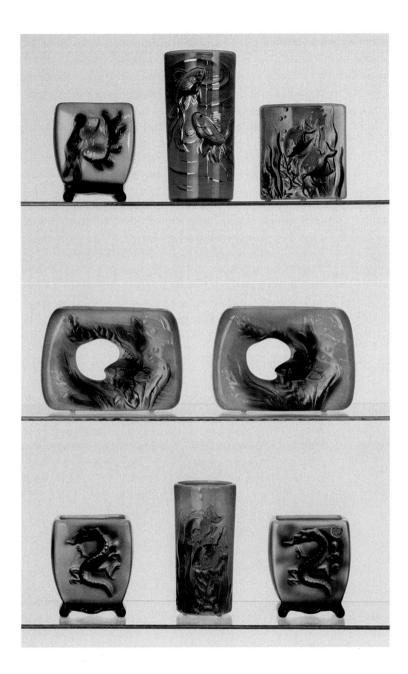

Royal Copley Items

Row 1: (a) 7½" Wide Brim Hat Girl Planter or Pocket. Signed with raised letters on the back. Made to hang or rest on a table. The big hat is chartreuse in color which is more difficult to find. Lips are puckered. Girl has right hand under right cheek. $40.00 – 45.00.

(b) 7½" Wide Brim Hat Boy Planter or Pocket. This is the mate to item (a) above. Lips are puckered. Boy has left hand under left cheek. Similar to the girl planter above. $40.00 – 45.00.

Row 2: (a) and (b) are identical to the Wide Brim Hat Girl and Boy in Row 1. The only difference is color. This pair is more likely to be found with blue hats. $35.00 – 40.00 each.

(c) 7½" Chinese Boy with Big Hat Planter or Pocket. Produced in very large quantities. Made to hang or rest on a table. Signed with raised letters on the back. Notice the boy has puckered lips whereas the girls below have smiling lips. The girl is found on page 67. $30.00 – 35.00.

Row 3: (a) and (b) 7½" Chinese Girl and Boy with Big Hat Planters or Pockets. The hats are a light gray. This is the color in which this pair is usually found. Again, notice the girl is smiling and the boy has his lips puckered. $24.00 – 28.00 each.

(c) and (d) The very same planters as (a) and (b) above but the hats are yellow and the clothing is dark green. Like all these planters they are signed with raised letters on the back and made to hang or rest on a table. $24.00 – 28.00 each.

Royal Copley Items

Row 1: (a) and (b) 8" Oriental Boy and Girl Planters with Large Basket on Back. Paper label only. $40.00 – 45.00 each.

(c) 7" Girl and Wheelbarrow Planter. Paper label only. Dress is a light green, hat is red, and wheelbarrow is dark green. $25.00 – 30.00.

Row 2: (a) and (b) 4¾" Oriental Children with Big Vase Planters. Paper label only. Included in the Lenox Assortment. Item (a) is sitting with clutched hands beside a teal colored urn or vase and item (b) is happily clutching a teal colored urn or vase with both hands and legs. The company identified item (a) as No. 71 and item (b) as No. 72. $12.00 – 15.00 each.

(c) The same item as item (a) but in a different color. Notice the writing on the face of the vase or urn. $12.00 – 15.00.

Row 3: (a) and (b) 7¾" Oriental Girl and Boy Planters with Basket on Ground. Item (a) is commonly referred to as the "pregnant lady" and item (b) as the "lantern boy." Signed with raised letters on the bottom. $15.00 – 20.00. each.

(c) and (d) The same planters but showing a change in color. Here the trousers are chartreuse and the upper part of the garment a dark green. On one of the color charts of the company the "pregnant lady" is identified as No. 15/1 and the "lantern boy" as No. 51/2. $15.00 – 20.00 each.

Royal Copley Items

Row 1: (a), (b), (c), (d), (e), and (f) 7½" Oriental Boy and Girl Figurines. Paper label only. We are showing the three colors in which they are usually found. On one of the company color charts the boy is identified as No. 42 and the girl as No. 41. One color is about as abundant as the other. The girl is harder to find. The center pair is yellow and green although the green doesn't show up very well. $20.00 – 24.00 each.

Row 2: (a) and (b) 6½" Farm Boy and Girl Planters. Signed with raised letters on the back. Notice that the boy has a fishing pole but the expression on his face seems to indicate that something else is a little more fascinating. This pair is shown in green and rose. So that we dare not be sexist let us say that the little girl may be encouraging a little time together. This is one of the delightful characteristics of Copley — capturing ideas, moods, and feelings. $30.00 – 35.00 each.
  (c) and (d) The same pair with the same characteristics but the color of the clothing is blue and yellow. $30.00 – 35.00 each.

Row 3: (a) and (b) 7½" Barefooted Boy and Girl Planters. Paper label only. This pair is sometimes referred to as the medium-sized hat planters. This pair of planters was included in the Carlton Assortment with the boy being identified as No. 82 and the girl as No. 81. Notice that the girl is smiling and the boy has his lips all puckered for some reason. $35.00 – 40.00 each.
  (c) and (d) The same pair with the same characteristics but the color of the clothing is reversed. $35.00 – 40.00 each.

Royal Copley Items

Row 1: (a) and (b) 5½" Oriental Girl and Boy Planters. Signed with raised letters on the bottom. Each is leaning on a vase or urn. The girl is on the left and the boy on the right. Colors are a rich rose and blue. Included in the Carlton Assortment with the girl listed as No. 61 and the boy as No. 62. $14.00 – 18.00 each.
(c) The same planter as item (b) above but in green and yellow. $14.00 – 18.00.

Row 2: (a) and (b) Girl and Boy Leaning on Barrel Planters. Paper label only. Girl is 6¼" and the boy is 6". Clothing is dark green and rose. $20.00 – 25.00 each.
(c) The same planter as shown in (a) but shown in a lovely dark blue. $20.00 – 25.00.

Row 3: (a) and (b) Dutch Boy and Girl with Bucket Planters. Paper label only. Each planter is a little over 6". Included in the Carlton Assortment with the boy bearing the No. 78 and the girl No. 79. $25.00 – 30.00 each.
(c) and (d) The same planters but shown in a different color. $25.00 – 30.00 each.

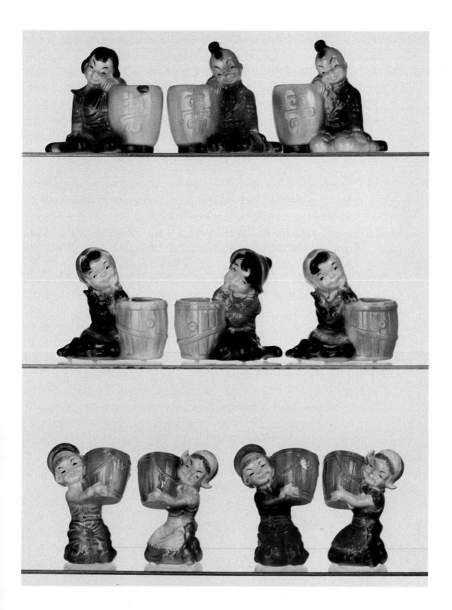

Royal Copley Items

Row 1: (a), (b), (c), and (d) 7" Pigtail Girl Planters. Signed with raised letters on the back. We are showing some of the colors in which this planter is found. Item (b) is more difficult to find. This planter was listed as No. 53 on one of the color charts of the company. Named in honor of Hildegard Lary of Westville, Illinois. (a), (c), (d) $35.00 – 40.00 each; (b) $50.00 – 60.00.

Row 2: (a) 7" Pigtail Girl Planter. This planter, shown in what collectors refer to as cobalt and yellow, is even harder to find than item (b) above in Row 1. $70.00 – 75.00.

(b) 8" Royal Copley Blackmoor Prince Planter/Wall Pocket. Signed with raised letters on the back. Harder to find than the two shown on next page. $40.00 – 45.00.

(c) 7½" Chinese Girl with Big Hat Planter/Wall Pocket. This is the mate to the boy shown on page 59. $30.00 – 35.00.

Row 3: (a) and (b) 8" Pirate Head Planters. Signed with raised letters on the back. Made to hang or rest on a table. Requires a little searching to find this item. The gray head covering is a bit harder to find than the pink or red. $45.00 – 50.00 each.

(c) 8¼ "Tony" Planter. Paper label only. Many names have been suggested for this special item. We are naming it in honor of Mr. Anthony Priolo who designed the item. We consider Anthony Priolo to be Spaulding's foremost designer. $70.00 – 75.00.

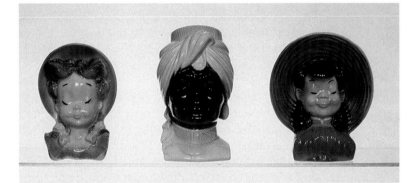

Royal Copley Items

Row 1: (a) and (b) 8½" Blackmoor Figurines. Paper label only. Designed as a pair. $25.00 – 30.00 each.

(c) 8½" Balinese Girl Planter. Paper label only. If there is a matching boy planter we haven't found it. $24.00 – 28.00.

Row 2: (a) and (b) 8" Large Angel Planters. Paper label only. Hard to find. We are naming these items big blue angel and big pink angel. We are naming the big blue angel in honor of Rick Summerlee and the big pink angel in honor of Daria Killinger of Michigan. $40.00 – 45.00 each.

(c) and (d) 6¼" Small Angel Planters. Paper label only. The little blue angel is easy to find but the little pink angel is hard to find. We are naming the little pink angel in honor of Nancy Peterson of Illinois and the little blue angel in honor of David Peterson of Illinois. All of the angels, big or small, are made to hang or rest on a table. (c) $30.00 – 35.00; (d) $35.00 – 40.00.

Row 3: (a) and (b) 8" Blackamoor Planters. Signed with raised letters on the back. Made to hang or rest on a table. Easy to find. Item (a) seems to be harder to find. (a) $40.00 – 45.00; (b) $30.00 – 35.00.

(c) and (d) 8" Colonial Old Man and Old Woman Planters. Signed with raised letters on the back and made to hang or rest on a table. These items represent some of the finest work done in Royal Copley. The Old Man is being reproduced in Japan but it can be easily spotted. $50.00 – 60.00 each.

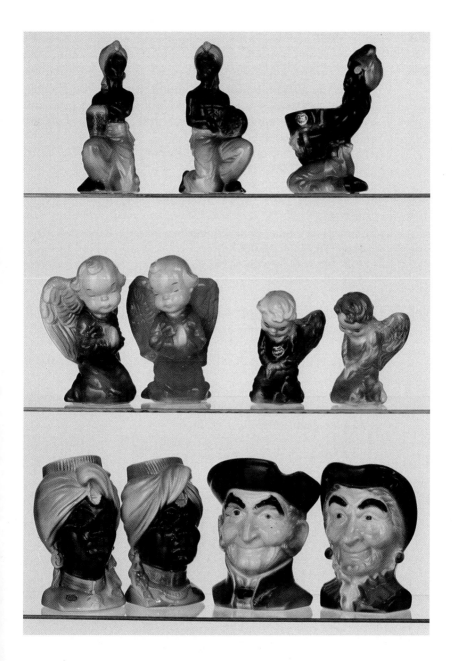

Royal Copley Items

Row 1: (a), (b), and (c) 6¼" Teddy Bear Planters. Paper label only. Item (a) is the most common color found. Item (b) is a chocolate brown which is very hard to find, and (c) is sort of a cinnamon color, not easily found. (a) and (c) $40.00 – 45.00 each; (b) $60.00 – 65.00.

(d) 5½" Teddy Bear onTree Stump Planter. Paper label only. Two runners. $20.00 – 25.00.

Row 2: (a) 7½" Teddy Bear Bank. Paper label only. Rare. $125.00 – 150.00.

(b) 7½" Teddy Bear with Concertina Planter. Paper label only. Rare. $85.00 – 95.00.

(c) 6¾" Teddy Bear with Mandolin Planter. Paper label only. Rare. $55.00 – 60.00.

Row 3: (a) 8" Teddy Bear Planter. Paper label only. Hard to find. Notice the open mouth with a sucker in the left hand. All bears are hard to find. $60.00 – 70.00.

(b) Same as item (a) but with a more realistic color. $60.00 – 70.00.

(c) 8¼" Bear Cub Clinging to Stump Planter. Paper label only. More easily found than the teddy bears. Notice the typical Copley stump. $35.00 – 40.00.

Royal Copley Items

Row 1: (a) and (b) 7⅜" Kitten Planters. These were part of the baby line. Shown in pink and blue. Hard to find. Found with a Royal Windsor label. $80.00 – 90.00 each.

(c) 6½" Kitten on Stump Planter. Paper label only. Kitten is gray with green eyes. $30.00 – 35.00.

Row 2: (a) 8" Kitten in Picnic Basket Planter. Paper label only. $70.00 – 75.00.

(b) 7½" Kitten in Cradle Planter. Paper label only. Cleverly designed. $100.00 – 125.00.

(c) 5¼" Black Cat and Tub Planter. Paper label only. This cat has all the appearance of a black cat on Halloween. $20.00 – 25.00.

Row 3: (a) 7½" Playful Kitten and Boot Planter. Paper label only. $50.00 – 55.00.

(b) 8" Kitten and Bird House Planter. Paper label only. $100.00 – 125.00.

(c) 8" Kitten and Moccasin Planter. Paper label only. Not easily found. The toe of the moccasin is hidden by the cat. $50.00 – 55.00.

Royal Copley Items

Row 1: (a) 7⅜" Kitten Planter. Like the planters shown on previous page, but with a different decal. $80.00 – 90.00.
(b) 6½" Kitten and Book Planter. Paper label only. Three runners. $30.00 – 35.00.
(c) 7½" Cat and Cello Planter. Paper label only. Hard to find. $100.00 – 125.00.

Row 2: (a) 6½" Kitten with Ball of Yarn Figurine. Very few with pink ball of yarn have been found. Paper label only. Too rare to price.
(b) 8¼" Kitten with Ball of Yarn Planter. Paper label only. The gold trim adds to the beauty of this rare item. Too rare to price.
(c) 8¼" Kitten with Ball of Yarn Planter. Paper label only. The yellow variation is easier to find. The gold-trimmed items are becoming very popular among collectors. $60.00 – 70.00.

Row 3: (a) and (b) 8¼" Kitten with Ball of Yarn Planters. Shown above in Row 2, but without the gold trim. (a) too rare to price; (b) $35.00 – 40.00.
(c) 6½" Kitten with Ball of Yarn Figurine. Paper label only. Easier to find with a yellow ball of yarn. $40.00 – 45.00.

Royal Copley Items

Row 1: (a) 5¾" Copley Dog Pulling Wagon. The word "Flyer" can be seen on the side of the wagon. Paper label only. Designed for use as a planter. $40.00 – 45.00.

(b) and (c) 5½" Cocker Spaniel with Basket Planters. Paper label only. Only difference is that of color. $20.00 – 25.00 each.

Row 2: (a), (b), and (c) 5¼" Posing Poodle with Bow Planters. Paper label only. Three runners. Hard to find. $45.00 – 50.00 each.

Row 3: (a) 7" Pup with Suitcase Planter. Paper label only. Notice the name tag that reads Skip. $45.00 – 50.00.

(b) 7" Pup in Basket Planter. Paper label only. Basket is a dark green. Notice the blanket. Sometimes found with a gaudy gold outline which was not done at the factory. $30.00 – 35.00.

(c) 7¾" Dog and Mail Box Planter. Paper label only. Notice the anxious waiting in the eyes and face of the dog. This is a reminder of how we felt at mail time while away at college or during WWII. We are naming this lovely item in honor of the person who first suggested we concentrate and prepare a book on Royal Copley, Mr. Ed Ashley, of Arcola, Illinois. $30.00 – 35.00.

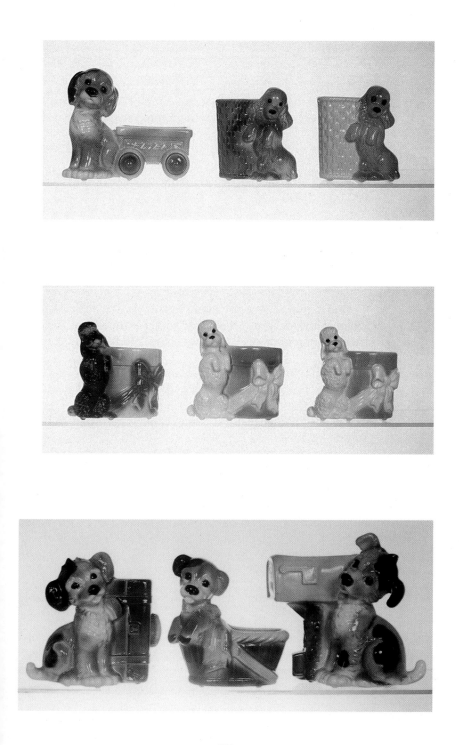

Royal Copley Items

Row 1: (a) 5" Cocker Head Planter/Wall Pocket. Signed with raised letters on the back. Notice that the head of item (b) was used to design this item. No. 66 in the Carlton Assortment. $28.00 – 34.00.

(b) 6¼" Cocker Spaniel Figurine. Paper label only. $20.00 – 25.00.

(c) 6" Spaniel Figurine. Paper label only. Collar around the neck. $20.00 – 25.00.

Row 2: (a) 6½" Dog Figurine. Paper label only. One of the items in the Oxford Assortment. Harder to find. $25.00 – 30.00.

(b) 7½" Dog Planter. The raised right foot makes this a more desirable item. Paper label only. Hard to find. $65.00 – 75.00.

(c) 8" Dog Figurine. Proper identification poses a problem as some of the dogs are definitely cocker spaniels and other a cocker or terrier cross. Paper label only. $30.00 – 35.00.

Row 3: (a) 8" Cocker Spaniel Planter. Paper label only. $30.00 – 35.00.

(b) 7" Cocker Spaniel Planter. Paper label only. A smaller version of item (c). Harder to find. $40.00 – 45.00.

(c) 8" Cocker Spaniel Planter. Paper label only. Three runners. $30.00 – 35.00.

Royal Copley Items

Row 1: (a) 8½" Mare and Foal Vase. One of the items found in the Oxford Assortment with a suggested value of $2.29 in 1952. Signed with raised letters on the bottom. This vase seems to capture the hearts of everyone who sees it. $30.00 – 35.00.
(b) and (c) 8" Horse with Mane Vases. Paper label only. Only difference is that of color. Designed by Anthony Priolo. (b) $30.00 – 35.00; (c) $50.00 – 55.00.

Row 2: (a) 7½" Large Elephant with Ball Planter. Lovely detail. Paper label only. $25.00 – 30.00.
(b) 6" Small Elephant with Ball Planter. Paper label only. Not as colorful as the large elephant. $20.00 – 25.00.
(c) 6½" Peter Rabbit Planter. Paper label only. $55.00 – 65.00.

Row 3: (a) 6¼" Horse Head Vase or Planter. Paper label only. Listed as No. 74 in the Lenox Assortment. $20.00 – 25.00.
(b) 4¾" Full Figure Grazing Horse Planter. Paper label only. Two runners. $28.00 – 32.00.
(c) 5¼" Pony Planter. Signed with raised letters on the back. Two runners. $12.00 – 15.00.

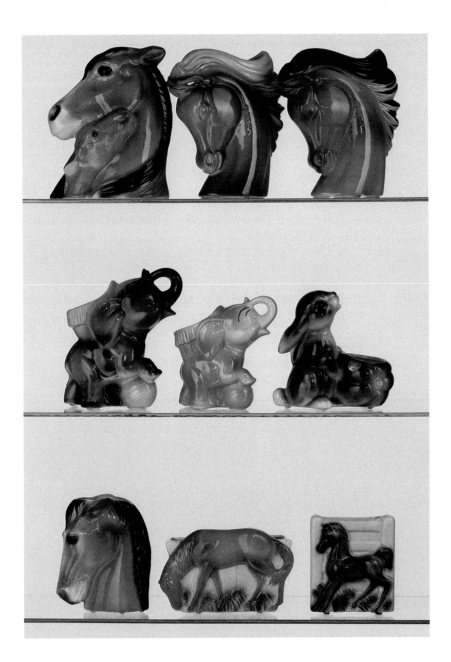

Royal Copley Items

Row 1: (a) and (b) 6" Deer and Fawn Rectangular Planters. Footed vases and planters are all the more desirable. Item (a) is beautifully outlined in gold. (a) $40.00 – 45.00; (b) $20.00 – 25.00.

(c) 6" Spaulding Deer on Rocker. This version with the fawn spots and gold trim is very hard to find. Found with a Spaulding label. Too rare to price.

Row 2: (a) 6½" Ram Head Planter. Unusual. Paper label only. $25.00 – 30.00.

(b) 8" Full Bodied Deer on Copley Stump Planter. Paper label only. $40.00 – 45.00.

(c) Little Deer Head Planter or Vase. Paper label only. Two runners. $25.00 – 30.00.

Row 3: (a) 9" Gazelle Vase Planter. No. 803 in the Oxford Assortment. Meticulously outlined in gold. Most are found without any gold. Signed with raised letters on the bottom. $40.00 – 45.00.

(b) 8½" Deer and Fawn Figurine. Signed with raised letters on the bottom. Figurines are harder to find. $40.00 – 45.00.

(c) 9" Deer and Fawn Planter. Signed and raised letters on the bottom. Notice that the planter is always taller than the corresponding figurine. $35.00 – 40.00.

Royal Copley Items

Row 1: (a) and (d) 7½" Large Pig Banks. Paper label and often a green stamp on item (a). Listed as No. 138 on one of the color charts of the company. Hard to find. Various color combinations can be found. Item (d) was made for the Park Natl. Bank of Newark, Ohio. Notice the word "Parky" on the front. Items made for special customers did not have paper labels as a rule. $75.00 – 85.00.

(b) 6" Middle-Size Pig Bank. Copley paper label but beneath it is a heart-shaped label with the words "Let me tuck your coins away for what you'll want to buy someday!" Listed as No. 37 on a company color chart. Color of stripes will vary. $50.00 – 60.00.

(c) 4½" Small Pig Bank. Color of stripes and basic color will vary. Paper label only. Hard to find. $50.00 – 55.00.

Row 2: (a), (b), (c), and (d) 6¼" Bow Tie Banks. Hard to find. Notice some have their eyes open, others closed. Paper label only. The hands can be seen in these pigs whereas the hands are clutched behind the pigs in Row 1. $45.00 – 50.00.

(e) 4½" Small Pig Bank. This bank can be found with the same kind of label as the 6" middle-sized pig bank. Harder to find. $50.00 – 55.00.

Row 3: (a), (b), (c), and (d) 7½" Large Pig Banks. Item (a) was made for the Midland's Buckeye Bank while (c) was a personalized item. All are hard to find without damage to coin slot or bottom holes enlarged to retrieve the coins. $75.00 – 85.00 each.

Royal Copley Items

Row 1: (a) and (b) 7" Large Hat Planters. Made to hang or rest on a table. Signed with raised letters on the back. Cleverly designed. One of the items found in the Oxford Assortment. The only difference between these planters is that of color. Item (a) has a yellow background whereas item (b) has a rose background. $40.00 – 45.00 each.

Row 2: (a), (b), and (c) 5½" Small Hat Planters. Made to hang or rest on a table. Signed with raised letters on the back. Listed as No. 65 in the Carlton Assortment. The only difference in these planters is that of color. Item (a) has a rose background, item (b) has a cobalt blue background, and item (c) has a tan background. $40.00 – 45.00 each.

Row 3: (a) 6½" x 11½" Jumping Salmon Planter. Paper label only. There are three rose colored salmon jumping over teal colored waves. Foam is white. A heavy item. This is a questionable item. NPA.

   (b) 4" Small Bowl with Perched Bird. Found in various colors. Green stamp on the bottom indicates it is one of the earlier items. Very common. Serves many uses. $12.00 – 14.00.

Royal Copley Items

Row 1: (a) and (b) 8" Dancing Lady Figurine Lamps. The firm that made the lamps shown on this page used Copley figurines mounted on appropriate metal bases. Very hard to find. Too rare to price.

Row 2: (a) and (e) 5" Leafy Ashtrays. Green stamp on bottom. Variation in color. $10.00 – 15.00 each.

(b) and (d) 7½" Oriental Boy and Girl Figure Lamps. The figurine was No. 42 on one of the color charts of the company. $75.00 – 85.00 each.

(c) 5" Bow and Ribbon Ashtray. Signed with raised letters on the bottom. Found in various colors with various sayings in the center of the tray. $40.00 – 45.00.

Royal Copley Items

Row 1: (a) and (d) 7½" Harmony Vases. Color is the only difference in these vases. Paper label only. Included in the Crown Assortment. $14.00 – 16.00 each.

(b) 6½" Harmony Large Planter. Paper label only. Included in the Crown Assortment. $12.00 – 15.00.

(c) 4½" Harmony Small Planter. Paper label only. Included in the Crown Assortment. $10.00 – 12.00.

Row 2: (a) 8½" Oval Homma Vase. Black background with white raised stem and leaves. Also found with a dark green background. Named in honor of Tom Homma of Villa Grove, Illinois. $16.00 – 18.00.

(b) 4" Round Triple Leaf Planter. Paper label only. The white leaves are found on either a black or dark green background. $14.00 – 16.00.

(c) 8¼" Stylized Leaf Vase. Paper label only. We are using the term "stylized" as many of these items were not designed to be botanically correct. Dr. Richard W. Pippen of Western Michigan University made the suggestion we use the term "stylized" to avoid any serious problem in identification. $12.00 – 15.00.

(d) 5½" Stylized Leaf Vase. Paper label only. Similar to item (c) above. $10.00 – 12.00.

Row 3: (a) and (b) 6½" Footed Bow and Ribbon Vases. Paper label only. The only difference is color. $14.00 – 18.00 each.

(c) 7½" Philodendron Footed Vase. Paper label only. $12.00 – 15.00.

(d) 4¼" Footed Philodendron Planter. Paper label only. $10.00 – 12.00.

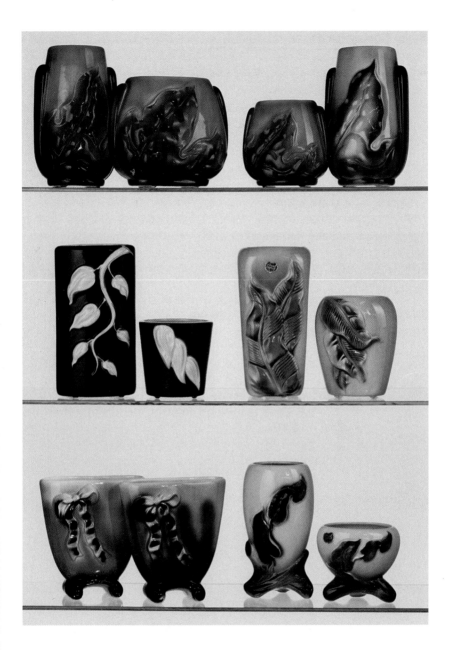

Royal Copley Items

Row 1: (a) 8½" Trailing Leaf and Vine Vase. Paper label only. $25.00 – 30.00.

(b) and (c) Black Floral Leaf and Stem items. Item (b) is a planter and item (c) is an 8" vase. Paper label only. (b) $10.00 – 12.00; (c) $14.00 – 18.00.

Row 2: (a) and (b) 7¼" Hardy Stem and Leaf Vases. Item (a) has a dark green background and item (b) a black background. $20.00 – 25.00 each.

(c) 4½" Double Spray Planter. Oval shape but pinched in at the top. Paper label only. $12.00 – 15.00.

Row 3: All items in Row 3 are Pink Dogwood items. All have paper labels.

(a) 8¼" Dogwood Vase. This is one of the floral patterns that is realistic. Prized highly. $20.00 – 24.00.

(b) 4½" Dogwood Plaque Planter. This planter was made for the florist trade. This item shows the Lord's Prayer but others can be found bearing various sayings and quotations. $20.00 – 25.00.

(c) 3½" Dogwood Oval Planter. $14.00 – 18.00.

(d) 4½" Small Oval Dogwood Planter. Beautifully designed. $12.00 – 15.00.

Royal Copley Items

Row 1: (a) and (b) 6" Bare Shoulder Lady Planters. Listed as No. 73 in the Lenox Assortment. Not difficult to find. Paper label only. The only difference in these planters is the color. Listed in honor of the Camargo Twp. Library in Villa Grove, Illinois. Nancy Jones, librarian, and Letha Wells and Chas. Knox. $50.00 – 60.00 each.

(c) and (d) 6" Gloved Lady Planters. Listed as No. 67 in the Carlton Assortment. Raised letters on the back of the planter. Harder to find than the Bare Shoulder Lady planter. The only difference in these planters is that of color. Named in honor of Barb White of Iowa. $50.00 – 60.00 each.

Row 2: (a), (b), and (c) are commonly referred to as the Dancing Lady. Height of 8". Seems to resemble Royal Doulton. It was listed as No. 43 on the company's color chart. Item (c) is the color that is hardest to find. (a) $100.00 – 125.00; (b) and (c) $125.00 – 150.00 each.

Row 3: (a) 6½" Indian Boy and Drum Planter. Paper label only. Easy to find. $20.00 – 25.00.

(b) 6" Elf and Shoe Planter. Paper label only. Shoe is a dark green. Hard to find. $35.00 – 40.00.

(c) 6" Elf and Stump Planter. Paper label only. Notice that the big stump is what we refer to as the Copley stump. It was used and carried over on many items. Hard to find. Red hat with dark green clothing. $35.00 – 40.00.

Royal Copley Items

Row 1: (a) 5½" Salt Box Planter/Wall Pocket. Signed with raised letters on the back. $35.00 – 40.00.

(b) 5½" Spice Box Planter/Wall Pocket with raised letters on the back. Very few have been found. A rare item. There are rumors of a Flour Box Planter/Wall Pocket that has been found. I have not seen one. $75.00 – 80.00.

Row 2: (a) and (b) 4½" Little Imagination Planters. Item (a) has a green background, whereas item (b) has a black background. Paper label only. $20.00 – 25.00 each.

(c) 5" Trailing Leaf and Vine Planter. Two runners. Paper label only. Hard to find. $20.00 – 25.00.

Row 3: (a) and (b) 4½" Royal Copley Harmony Planters. This is the pattern that collectors refer to as tri-color. There are two color variations. The larger leaf will either be solid pink or a yellow-orange color like item (b). Notice how the gold outlining adds to the beauty of item (b). (a) $40.00 – 45.00; (b) $60.00 – 70.00.

(c) 7½" Harmony Vase. Paper label only. The tri-color variation is very hard to find. $50.00 – 55.00.

Royal Copley Items

Row 1: (a), (b), and (c) 6¼" Water Lily Planters. Item (a) is the color most commonly found. Item (b) shows how the gold trim adds to the beauty of this planter. Item (c) with its gray background and pink water lilies is very hard to find. (a) $20.00 – 25.00; (b) $40.00 – 45.00; (c) $70.00 – 75.00.

Row 2: (a) 7½" Deer and Doe Planter. A color variation rarely seen. $45.00 – 50.00.
  (b) 7½" Resting Doe and Fawn Planter. Although this planter has not been confirmed as being Copley, it has all the characteristics. NPA.

Row 3: (a) 6" Running Horse Planter. Paper label only. Easier to find. The horse appears on one side only. $15.00 – 20.00.
  (b) 7½" Deer and Doe Planter. This is the color commonly found. Paper label only. $15.00 – 20.00.
  (c) 6" Running Gazelles Planter. Paper label only. Notice that all animals shown in Row 3 are in relief. $15.00 – 20.00.

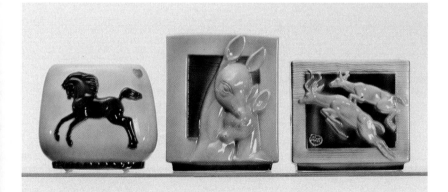

99

Royal Copley Items

Row 1: (a) 4½" Royal Copley Vase. Pink background with robin's egg blue specks. "U.S.A" impressed on the bottom. $8.00 – 10.00.

(b) 12½" x 4¾" Boat-shaped Planter. Marked "U.S.A." impressed, turquoise with brown specks. $14.00 – 16.00.

Row 2: (a) 8" Royal Copley Vase. Pink and brown with white blotches. "U.S.A" impressed. $8.00 – 10.00.

(b) 3½" Boat-shaped Planter. Yellow with rose colored specks. "U.S.A" impressed. $8.00 – 10.00.

(c) 6½" Royal Copley Vase. White with rose specks. "U.S.A" impressed. $8.00 – 10.00.

Row 3: (a) 6" Parallel Rays Variation Planter. Decorated like Row 2 (a) above. "U.S.A" impressed. $10.00 – 12.00.

(b) 7½" Parallel Rays Variation Planter. Yellow and brown with white blotches. "U.S.A." impressed. $10.00 – 12.00.

(c) 7" Royal Copley Comma Vase. Presence of three runners. Paper label only. Can be found in three different sizes and two color variations. $16.00 – 18.00.

Royal Copley Items

Row 1: (a), (b), and (c) are three different design variations of metal plant holders known as Royal Copley Iron Craft. As you can see, they all have leaves incorporated into the design. They were produced for the ribbed and "plain Jane" planters. $20.00 – 25.00 each.

Row 2: Item (b) above has been turned to show the original name and price tags. It is unknown as to whether Spaulding may have made these accessory items or if they were purchased from a metals manufacturing firm.

Royal Windsor Items

Top Row: Framed Royal Windsor Mallard Duck. When we visited Margaret Kadisch, former decorator for Spaulding, she loaned us a brochure that has proven to be very valuable in our research. The company produced three pairs of Royal Windsor Ducks and they were referred to as Game Birds of America. They were a series. The lovely Mallard shown in this picture happens to be No. 496 in the series with its mate having the No. 495. It was drawn and colored by Joan Priolo. Although the Priolos lived in New Jersey, they sent sketches to be approved every two weeks. We are so glad to have an example of what was done before an item was put into production.

Bottom: (a) and (b) Large Royal Windsor Mallards. This pair is one of three pairs of ducks comprising the Game Birds of North America series. They are found with a Royal Windsor label and have their designer's name, A. D. Priolo, at the edge of the base. $175.00 – 200.00 pair.

Spaulding Items

Row 1: (a) 4¼" Spaulding Miss Piggie Creamer. This one is not marked. No more than six of these creamers have been reported. It would be pure speculation to say why so few have been found. It is my opinion, for what it is worth, that it was redesigned into the Pig creamers shown in items (b) and (c). Too rare to price.

(b) and (c) 4½" Spaulding Pig Creamer. "Pat. Pending" on the bottom or Spaulding Pat. 113726. Only difference is color variation. $24.00 – 28.00 each.

Row 2: (a) 4¼" Spaulding Miss Piggie Creamer. This one is marked "Patent Pending." Too rare to price.

(b) 4¾" Spaulding Chick Creamer. Decorated in various colors. Found with a Spaulding label. $24.00 – 28.00.

(c) 4½" Spaulding Duck Creamer. Only difference is color variation. $24.00 – 28.00.

Row 3: (a) and (b) 4¾" Spaulding Chick Creamers. Easy to find. Decorated in various colors. Found with "Pat. Pending" or "Spaulding Pat. 113724" on the bottom. We are naming this lovely item in honor of Rena London of Texas. $24.00 – 28.00.

(c) and (d) 4½" Spaulding Duck Creamers. Easy to find. Found in a variety of colors. Found with "Pat. Pending" or "Spaulding Pat. 113725" on the bottom. Notice the cane under the wing which provides a more novel tail. $24.00 – 28.00.

Spaulding Items

Row 1: (a) 8½" Spaulding Decal Lamp Base. It has four sides each with a frame around the flower decal. $30.00 – 35.00.

(b) 8½" Spaulding Tulip Decal Lamp Base. This lamp base has four petals, each with a flower decal. $35.00 – 40.00.

(c) 8½" Spaulding Decal Lamp Base. This lamp base has a stylized bird's neck on both sides, coming down from the top. $50.00 – 55.00.

(d) 8½" Spaulding Decal Lamp Base. There are flowers with gold trim on the sides of this lamp base. $35.00 – 40.00.

Row 2 (a) 10½" Spaulding Decal Lamp Base. A very lovely lamp with beaded handles. $45.00 – 50.00.

(b) and (c) 10½" Spaulding Lamp Bases. Only difference is the flower decals. $45.00 – 50.00 each.

Row 3: (a) 5¼" Spaulding Boot. This is the small-sized boot vase. $20.00 – 25.00.

(b) 7¼" Spaulding Boot. Spaulding made three sizes, with this one being the middle-sized one. $30.00 – 35.00.

(c) 9¼" Spaulding Boot. Each one has a yellow tulip on one side and a pink tulip on the opposite side. This is the only pattern that was done. $40.00 – 45.00.

108

Some of Spaulding's Special People

Morris Feinberg
President
The Spaulding China Company
1941 – 1957

Mr. and Mrs. Wolfe dedicated this book to Mr. Feinberg.

PRESENTED TO
MORRIS FEINBERG, PRES.
DANIEL EISENBERG, V. PRES.
DAVID BOROWITZ, V. PRES.
IRVING MILLER, SEC'Y.·TREAS.
OFFICERS OF SPAULDING CHINA COMPANY
BY THEIR EMPLOYEES
IN APPRECIATION OF
THEIR UNTIRING EFFORTS IN OUR BEHALF
PRESENTED DECEMBER 10, 1946

This plaque is one of the cherished mementos that used to hang on the wall of the Spaulding China Company.

Morris Feinberg: 1900 – 1982
"The Heart and Soul of Spaulding"

Morris Feinberg was born January 25, 1900, in Long Island, New York.

He excelled in school, in sports, and in fact in everything he attempted. He entered business at twenty with a partner, Irving Miller, importing various household items from Europe. At night he attended New York University gaining a degree in business administration.

On October 31, 1929, Morris married Ida Kuropatkin and in May of 1931 their only child, a son, Joe, was born.

In the middle thirties Morris and Irving began to design, assemble, and sell pottery kitchen clocks throughout the United States. They produced the clocks for Sears Roebuck under the Harmony House label.

Needing ceramic parts for clocks. Mr. Feinberg made a trip to Sebring, Ohio, a likely center for such needs. While there, the idea of manufacturing artware pottery became more than a dream. Early in 1941 the partners bought a defunct plant in Sebring to begin their own production of artware pottery. It took unusual courage for a stranger from New York to establish a major plant in Sebring. But it wasn't long until he became highly respected for his business ability and for the simple humanity he practiced as a person.

In 1957, due to adverse trends and changing conditions, Morris retired and decided to sell out. For the next five years he devoted himself to his investments in the stock market and golf.

In 1962 he joined L. M. Rosenthal, an investment banking firm, as the senior advisor. For the next ten years he enjoyed this second act in his business life.

In 1972 he retired from business for the second time and moved permanently to Key Biscayne, Florida.

The last ten years were filled with doing the things he and his lovely wife, Ida, enjoyed so very much. Although this is the story of the life of Morris Feinberg, we must not fail to mention Ida Feinberg, a lady of rare design. Although she remained in the background, she was without a doubt a source of inspiration that gave encouragement to every move and decision that was made.

Through the 82 years of his life he gained the love and respect of many people because of his keen intellect, warmth, and sense of humor.

The family as a unit was always his top priority. His perpetual youth and constant optimism were an inspiration to all.

On August 22, 1982, Morris Feinberg died following an accidental fall at his home four days earlier. His last correspondence with me on

Morris Feinberg: 1900 – 1982

August 15 ends with these words:
    "I am very gratified that posterity is rewarding the creative efforts and high standards that were lavished on Spaulding's production."

After Glow

I'd like the memory of me
    to be a happy one.
I'd like to leave an afterglow
    of smiles when life is done.

I'd like to leave an echo
    whispering softly down the ways,
Of happy times and laughing times
    and bright and sunny days.

I'd like the tears of those who grieve,
    to dry before the sun
Of happy memories that I leave
    When life is done

Carol Mirkel

James G. Eardley
Spaulding's Man of the Hour

Only rarely does a man like James G. Eardley appear. Here was a man destined from the beginning to be a potter among potters. His grandfather emigrated to the United States from Burslem, England, near Stoke-on-Trent, the chief pottery center in England. And his father, Samuel L. Eardley, was the first treasurer of the National Potter's Union when it was organized in the late 1880s or early 1890s in East Liverpool, Ohio.

James Eardley joined Spaulding China Company when it began operation in 1942 and remained with the company until it was finally liquidated. It would take pages to enumerate all the facets of his busy, worthwhile, and outstanding life. He was a prominent churchman, a highly respected businessman, a man known as Mr. Republican in Mahoning County, a three-time delegate to the Republican National Convention, a 32nd degree Mason, and a veteran of World War I.

His chief contribution to Spaulding was his thorough knowledge of the pottery industry. He was a skilled administrator and organizer without whose leadership the story of Spaulding would have been less prominent. Few administrators were loved and appreciated as much as James G. Eardley. We can say without reservation he was Spaulding's man of the hour.

He passed away on July 3, 1973, at the age of eighty. His devoted widow, Ruth Hall Eardley, and his daughter, Charlotte H. Eardley, make their home in Berea, Ohio.

Anthony Priolo: 1922 – 1991
Designer Deluxe

Many factors have contributed to the popularity and desirability of Royal Copley. Without a doubt it was design more than anything else that played the biggest role in bringing Royal Copley to the scene as one of our latest collectibles.

From 1949 to 1955 some of Spaulding's finest work was conceived and designed. This period of time might be referred to as Spaulding's finest hour. Collectors, invariably, in viewing a collection of Royal Copley, are quick to agree that the Priolo items are the most creative and novel of all.

Spaulding items, although beautifully done, were mass produced at a special price for special customers. In no way did these items compare with the fine figurines and art work of the Gort China Company of Metuchen, New Jersey, where Priolo worked before beginning his work at Spaulding.

A brief description of Anthony Priolo's life and work will give us a glimpse of why he was a "designer deluxe" in every sense of the word. After graduating from Westfield High School, he was inducted into the United States Army in 1943 and served in the Pacific. After his discharge in 1946, he went to the American School of Design in New York City where he received his camouflage degree (this was his job in the army). In late 1946 he started designing for Gort Bone China producing very expensive figurines. In 1949 be began his work at Spaulding.

When Spaulding shut down, he was invited to work for G. Perlmutter Associates, a firm specializing in the design of furniture and household items.

He and his family moved to California in 1961 where he started his own ceramic business. He stopped doing ceramics when the move was made to Santa Barbara in 1966.

From 1967 to 1981 he specialized in the design of fine jewelry and also taught the sculpture of jewelry at Santa Barbara City College. He is now retired from teaching and commercial jewelry and spending his time with his own sculpture in bronze, wood, and ceramics. He works out of his own shop in Santa Barbara.

His lovely wife, Joan, is no stranger to the field of art and design. One of the very lovely sketches shown in this book is that of a Royal Windsor Mallard Duck. It was from this sketch that the item was approved for mass production. You will notice that the sketch is personally signed by her. We are honored to show a glimpse of her outstanding and creative work.

Anthony Priolo — Designer Deluxe

Truly, Anthony Priolo was Spaulding's foremost designer and deserves the title designer deluxe.

Margaret Kadisch: 1904 – 1998
The Lady Whose Fascination
with Color Has Touched Us All!

Many people contributed to the successful operation at Spaulding. We wish we could take the time to mention all the names and all the people who made significant contributions to the story of Spaulding. Time has taken its toll and therefore we are going to have to give a blanket thanks to all those wonderful people who added so much to the glory that belonged to Spaulding.

We had the rare privilege of visiting with Miss Kadisch in her home at Sebring, Ohio, in October 1981. Her contribution to Spaulding was recognized and deeply appreciated by all who knew her and worked with her. She was in charge of the decorating department at Spaulding from the late 1940s until 1957. It is obvious from all the lovely items produced that she possessed a rare and gifted talent. We will remember her each time we behold the beauty of Royal Copley.

ROYAL COPLEY DECORATIVE CERAMIC ARTWARE

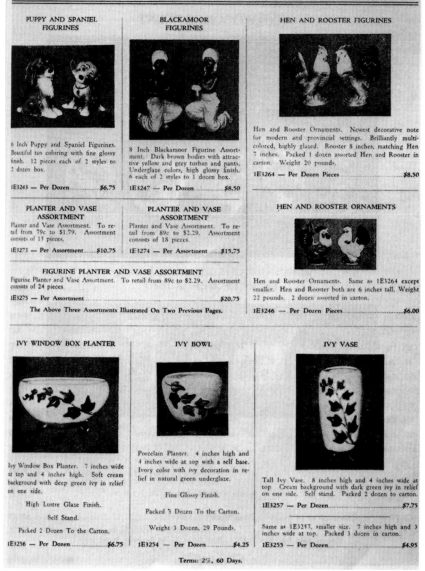

PUPPY AND SPANIEL FIGURINES

6 Inch Puppy and Spaniel Figurines. Beautiful tan coloring with fine glossy finish. 12 pieces each of 2 styles to 2 dozen box.

1E3243 — Per Dozen $6.75

BLACKAMOOR FIGURINES

8 Inch Blackamoor Figurine Assortment. Dark brown bodies with attractive yellow and grey turban and pants. Underglaze colors, high glossy finish. 6 each of 2 styles to 1 dozen box.

1E3247 — Per Dozen $8.50

HEN AND ROOSTER FIGURINES

Hen and Rooster Ornaments. Newest decorative note for modern and provincial settings. Brilliantly multi-colored, highly glazed. Rooster 8 inches, matching Hen 7 inches. Packed 1 dozen assorted Hen and Rooster in carton. Weight 20 pounds.

1E3264 — Per Dozen Pieces $8.50

PLANTER AND VASE ASSORTMENT

Planter and Vase Assortment. To retail from 79c to $1.79. Assortment consists of 15 pieces.

1E3273 — Per Assortment $10.75

PLANTER AND VASE ASSORTMENT

Planter and Vase Assortment. To retail from 89c to $2.29. Assortment consists of 18 pieces.

1E3274 — Per Assortment $15.75

FIGURINE PLANTER AND VASE ASSORTMENT

Figurine Planter and Vase Assortment. To retail from 89c to $2.29. Assortment consists of 24 pieces.

1E3275 — Per Assortment $20.75

The Above Three Assortments Illustrated On Two Previous Pages.

HEN AND ROOSTER ORNAMENTS

Hen and Rooster Ornaments. Same as 1E3264 except smaller. Hen and Rooster both are 6 inches tall. Weight 22 pounds. 2 dozen assorted in carton.

1E3246 — Per Dozen Pieces $6.00

IVY WINDOW BOX PLANTER

Ivy Window Box Planter. 7 inches wide at top and 4 inches high. Soft cream background with deep green ivy in relief on one side.

High Lustre Glaze Finish.

Self Stand.

Packed 2 Dozen To the Carton.

1E3256 — Per Dozen $6.75

IVY BOWL

Porcelain Planter. 4 inches high and 4 inches wide at top with a self base. Ivory color with ivy decoration in relief in natural green underglaze.

Fine Glossy Finish.

Packed 3 Dozen To the Carton.

Weight 3 Dozen, 29 Pounds.

1E3254 — Per Dozen $4.25

Terms: 2%, 60 Days.

IVY VASE

Tall Ivy Vase. 8 inches high and 4 inches wide at top. Cream background with dark green ivy in relief on one side. Self stand. Packed 2 dozen to carton.

1E3257 — Per Dozen $7.75

Same as 1E3257, smaller size. 7 inches high and 3 inches wide at top. Packed 3 dozen in carton.

1E3255 — Per Dozen $4.95

Used with permission of Betty Bell of Verona, Mississippi, and Nora Koch, editor of the *Depression Glass Daze*, Otisville, Michigan.

OXFORD ASSORTMENT

Packing: Single Carton Containing 24 Pieces As Follows:

No.	Description	Size	Quantities	Suggested Retail Each	
F24	Dog Figurine	6½ Inches	4 Only	$ .89	$ 3.
F25	Kitten Figurine	6½ Inches	3 Only	.89	2.
40	Hat Planter	7 Inches	3 Only	1.19	3.
41	Teddy Bear Planter	8 Inches	2 Only	1.19	2.
F42	Duck Figurine	7¼ Inches	2 Only	1.19	2.
F603	Dog Figurine	8 Inches	2 Only	1.39	2.
803	Gazelle Vase Planter	9 Inches	2 Only	1.89	3.
804	Kitten Planter	8¼ Inches	2 Only	1.89	3.
805	Fruit Plate Planter	6¾ Inches	2 Only	1.89	3.
901	Mare and Foal Vase	8½ Inches	2 Only	2.29	4.
			24 Pieces		$33

Weight 36 Pounds Packed

1E3275 — Per Assortment of 24 Pieces — From Stock .... $20.

Illustrated Retail Price Sheet Packed In Every Carton To Aid Retailer In Pricing Items

Terms: 2%, 60 Days.

Used with permission of Betty Bell of Verona, Mississippi, and Nora Koch, editor of the *Depression Glass Daze*, Otisville, Michigan.

CROWN ASSORTMENT

Packing: Single Carton Containing 15 Pieces As Follows:

No.	Description	Size	Quantities	Suggested Retail Each	Suggested Retail Total
	Harmony Small Planter	4½ Inches	6 Only	$ .79	$ 4.74
	Harmony Vase	7½ Inches	4 Only	1.19	4.76
	Harmony Window-Box	4½ Inches	3 Only	1.39	4.17
	Harmony Large Planter	6½ Inches	2 Only	1.79	3.58
			15 Pieces		$17.25

Weight 20 Pounds Packed

1E32"3 — Per Assortment of 15 Pieces — From Stock..................................$10.75

ESSEX ASSORTMENT

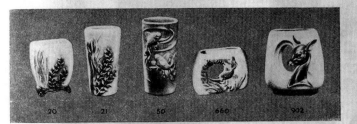

Packing: Single Carton Containing 18 Pieces As Follows:

No.	Description	Size	Quantities	Suggested Retail Each	Suggested Retail Total
20	Marine Planter	5½ Inches	6 Only	$ .89	$ 5.34
21	Marine Vase	7 Inches	4 Only	.89	3.56
50	Fish Column Vase	8 Inches	2 Only	1.29	2.58
660	Open Fish Vase-Planter	5½ Inches	3 Only	1.89	5.67
902	Deer Open Vase-Planter	7½ Inches	3 Only	2.29	6.87
			18 Pieces		$24.0

Weight 29 Pounds Packed

1E32"4 — Per Assortment of 18 Pieces — From Stock...............................$15.7

Illustrated Retail Price Sheet Packed In Every Carton To Aid Retailer In Pricing Items

Terms: 2%, 60 Days.

Used with permission of Betty Bell of Verona, Mississippi, and Nora Koch, editor of the *Depression Glass Daze*, Otisville, Michigan.

ROYAL COPLEY PLANTERS

PLANTER OR FLOWER VASE

Porcelain Planter or Flower Vase. 5½ inches high x 4½ inches wide at top. Fish design in relief on one side. Gorgeous blend of maroon, grey and navy blue under fine glossy finish. Self base. 2 dozen in a box.

1E3258 — Per Dozen................$6.00

PIRATE HEAD PLANTER

Pirate Planter. 8 inches high x 5½ inches wide. Something different. Two-color combinations assorted, red with green and grey with yellow. Natural color face. Packed 1 dozen to the carton.

1E3250 — Per Dozen................$13.25

WATER LILY PLANTER

Porcelain Planter. 6½ inches high x 5 inches wide. Water lilies in relief on one side. Beautiful chartreuse, white, deep green and blue color combinations with highly glazed finish. 1 dozen in a box.

1E3259 — Per Dozen................$10.50

BALINESE GIRL PLANTER

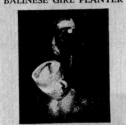

Balinese Girl Planter. Unusually attractive item, richly colored. 8 inches high x 5 inches wide. Dark brown body with grey and green blending into a beautiful combination on turban and pants. Packed 1 dozen to the carton.

1E3248 — Per Dozen................$11.50

HEN AND ROOSTER

Hen and Rooster Planter. Five brilliant colors, fired underglaze. Rooster 8 inches high, Hen slightly smaller. 1 dozen in carton.

1E3269 — Per Dozen Pieces..........$13.25

BLACKAMOOR PLANTER

Porcelain Planter or Flower Vase for table or wall, 8 inches high x 5 inches wide. Black face, white and yellow turban. Underglaze colors, high glossy finish. 1 dozen in carton. Weight 1 dozen, 18 pounds.

1E3249 — Per Dozen................$11.50

DUCK PLANTER

Large gracefully designed Duck with open top, brightly multi-colored, fine glossy finish. 8 inches high x 9 inches long. 1 dozen in a carton.

1E3266 — Per Dozen................$11.50

ROOSTER PLANTER

Rooster Planter. 7¼ inches high. 2 dozen in a carton.

1E3267 — Per Dozen................$7.75

DOUBLE FAWN PLANTER

Double Fawn Planter. 9¾ inches high x 5½ inches wide at base. Beautiful high gloss finish over rich two-tone brown. Packed 1 dozen in carton.

1E3251 — Per Dozen................$14.95

Terms: 2%, 60 Days.

Royal Copley (DECORATIVE ARTWARE)

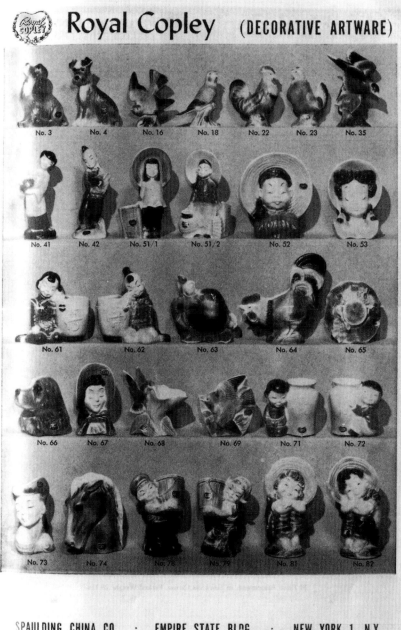

No. 3   No. 4   No. 16   No. 18   No. 22   No. 23   No. 35

No. 41   No. 42   No. 51/1   No. 51/2   No. 52   No. 53

No. 61   No. 62   No. 63   No. 64   No. 65

No. 66   No. 67   No. 68   No. 69   No. 71   No. 72

No. 73   No. 74   No. 78   No. 79   No. 81   No. 82

SPAULDING CHINA CO. · EMPIRE STATE BLDG. · NEW YORK 1. N.Y.

121

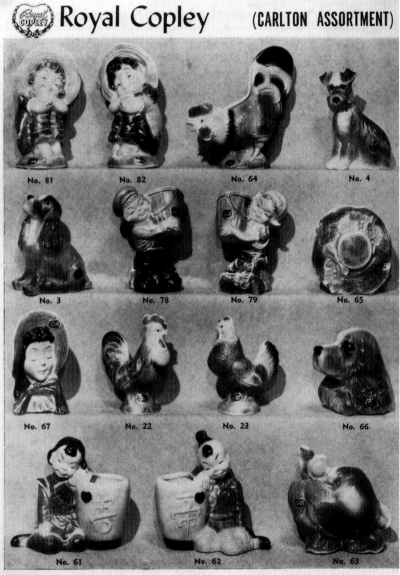

No. 81   No. 82   No. 64   No. 4

No. 3   No. 78   No. 79   No. 65

No. 67   No. 22   No. 23   No. 66

No. 61   No. 62   No. 63

24 Piece Assortment, in Strawless Carton, Packed Weight 28 Lbs.

Courtesy of Margaret Kadisch, Sebring, Ohio.

"Life gives nothing to men without great labor."
— Horace

"A thing of beauty is a joy forever."
— Keats

"An artist lives everywhere."
— Fr.

"Lives of great men
all remind us,
We can make our lives
sublime.
And departing, leave
behind us
Footprints on the sands
of time."
— Longfellow

Bibliography and Source Material

Reprints from a 1952 wholesale catalog showing Royal Copley. *Depression Glass Daze*, June 1979. Used with permission of Betty Bell of Verona, Mississippi, and Nora Koch, editor of the *Depression Glass Daze*, Otisville, Michigan.

Personal correspondence with Mrs. James G. Eardley and Charlotte H. Eardley, Berea, Ohio, 1981 and 1982.

Original color charts from the Spaulding China Co., courtesy of Morris Feinberg, Key Biscayne, Florida.

Personal interview with Morris Feinberg, June 7, 1982, at his home in Key Biscayne, Florida.

Personal correspondence and phone conversations with Morris Feinberg, 1981 and 1982.

Phone conversations and personal correspondence with Joe Feinberg, son of Morris Feinberg, September and October 1982.

Personal interview with Margaret Kadisch, Sebring, Ohio, October 1981.

Personal correspondence and phone conversations with Margaret Kadisch, Sebring, Ohio, 1992.

An original brochure showing many items made by the Spaulding China Company, courtesy of Margaret Kadisch.

Lois Lehner, "American Dinnerware and Commercial Pottery," *Depression Glass Daze*, September 1979.

Rena London, Richardson, Texas. Copies of Patents on Pig and Duck Figurines designed by Irving Miller in 1945.

Rena London, Richardson, Texas. Photo of Royal Copley, clips, and personal correspondence, October 1982.

Betty Newbound, Union Lake, Michigan. Article on Royal Copley, *Depression Glass Daze*, August 1982.

Personal correspondence and phone conversations with Anthony Priolo, Santa Barbara, California, 1982, 1990.

Sebring, Ohio: A Brief History of Sebring's 50th Anniversary, Library, Sebring, Ohio. 1949.

Phone conversations with Harry Runyon, former Spaulding China employee, Sebring, Ohio, 1994.

Acknowledgments and Appreciation

There is no way to adequately thank people who have given so generously of their time and effort in our behalf. The following people are deserving of any words of thanks we can offer. It was their help, encouragement, and personal interest that made this book possible. If the book has any merit the credit rightfully belongs to them.

Alabama – James Ellett.

California – Richard and Linda Guffey, and Anthony and Joan Priolo.

Florida – Barbara Burke, Joe Feinberg, Morris Feinberg, and Tanya Green.

Illinois – Ed Ashley, Gladys Collier, Louie Ella Davis, Carol De Moss, Gene Ellison, Jim and Betty Frink, Ruby Gano, Dr. George Godfrey, Wm. Goff, Jan Granse, Judy Hudson, Dr. Lawrence B. Hunt, Inez Jenkins, Virginia and Lawrence Keefe, Hildegard Lary, Cathy LeGrand, Ed Lohr, Dee Long, Charles Lumsdon, Eileen Mullen, Dorothy Moody, Chris Morrow, Dr. Iain Paul, and David and Nancy Peterson.

Indiana – Elizabeth and Chas. Boyce, Ted Haun, and Sharon and Bob Huxford.

Iowa – Laura Erickson, Glenn Hovinga, Geneva Ives, Kevin and Marilyn Stein, and Warren and Barb White.

Kansas – Lloyd and Alda Evans.

Kentucky – Dana Curtis.

Michigan – Don Brewer, Daria Killinger, Norma Killinger, Nora Koch, Betty Newbound, Dr. Richard W. Pippen, Larry Robinson, Linda Smith, and Rick Summerlee.

Missouri – Dave and Mary Boylan, Roy Wooldridge, Juarine Wooldridge.

Mississippi – Betty Bell.

Nebraska – Rose and Jim Huffman, and Bob and Judy Mohnike.

New York – Harvey Duke, and Ed Gisel.

Ohio – Frank Barrett, Betty and Floyd Carson, Linley Carson, Shirley Charney, Delores Drown, Charlotte H. Eardley, Mrs. James G. Eardley, Shirley Graff, Margaret Kadisch, Paul Nowack, Harry Runyon, and Lillian Szafranski.

Oregon – Ron Perrick.

Pennsylvania – Dennis Zerby.